CELEBRATION IN SONG

copyright 1983 by Christian Publications, Inc., Camp Hill, PA 17011-8870

ISBN: 0-87509-333-7

Printed in the United States of America

The *Introduction Markings* used in this hymnal are the property of Christian Publications and are covered under the copyright of this entire published work.

Acknowledgment

Grateful acknowledgment is given to those who have granted permission for the use of their hymns and tunes. Every effort has been made to properly accredit these in the body of the book. If through inadvertence, any omissions occur, upon written notification, acknowledgment will be included in future editions.

Christian Publications, Inc.

3825 Hartzdale Drive, Camp Hill, PA 17011-8870

CELEBRATION

Music has always been associated with God's people. Moses sang when God delivered the Hebrews from Egypt. When the Ark of the Covenant was brought back to Israel (1 Chronicles 16), David ordered a great choir and an orchestra to celebrate the occasion and sing praises unto the Lord. The people sang as they went to Jerusalem, recounting God's blessings and His dealings with them, joyfully praising Him for all His wondrous works. Singers were among the first to return from exile in Persia for the rebuilding of the Temple. Mary lifted her praise to God, and angels rejoiced at the Saviour's birth. Simeon blessed God that the Messiah had at last appeared.

We today who have been redeemed and who love God join with the multitudes throughout the centuries who have sung praises to the Lord, rejoicing in His mighty works. We celebrate His goodness, His mercy, His love and His truth.

Let us unite to tell the world of this great God whom we adore. We look forward to that day of celebration when men out of every tribe and nation shall join in that great chorus: "Blessing, and honour, and glory, and power, be unto Him that sitteth upon the throne, and unto the Lamb for ever and ever" (Revelation 5:13).

Presidents of The Christian and Missionary Alliance

Albert B. Simpson
Founder
1887–1919

Paul Rader
1920–1923

Frederic H. Senft
1924–1925

Harry M. Shuman
1926–1953

Harry L. Turner
1954–1959

Nathan Bailey
1960–1978

Louis L. King
1978–

**President, C&MA in Canada*

*Melvin P. Sylvester**
1981–

Saying with a loud voice, Worthy is the Lamb that was slain to receive power, and riches, and wisdom, and strength, and honour, and glory, and blessing. . . . Blessing, and honour, and glory, and power, be unto him that sitteth upon the throne, and unto the Lamb for ever and ever. (Rev. 5:12-13)

Rejoice, Ye Pure in Heart 1

Rejoice evermore. . . . In everything give thanks . . 1 Thess. 5:16, 18

MARION S.M. with Refrain
Arthur H. Messiter, 1834-1916

Edward H. Plumptre, 1821-1891

1. Re - joice, ye pure in heart, Re - joice, give thanks, and sing;
2. Bright youth and snow-crowned age, Strong men and maid - ens fair,
3. With all the an - gel choirs, With all the saints on earth,
4. Yes, on through life's long path, Still chant - ing as ye go;
5. Still lift your stand - ard high, Still march in firm ar - ray;

Your fes - tal ban - ner wave on high, The cross of Christ your King.
Raise high your free, ex - ult - ing song, God's won-drous praise de - clare.
Pour out the strains of joy and bliss, True rap-ture, no-blest mirth!
From youth to age, by night and day, In glad-ness and in woe.
As war - riors through the dark - ness toil Till dawns the gold- en day.

REFRAIN
Re-joice, re - joice, Re - joice, give thanks, and sing! A - MEN.
Re - joice, re - joice,

Glory Be to God

. . . the Father, the Word, and the Holy Ghost: and these three are one. 1 John 5:7

Horatius Bonar, 1808-1889

REGENT SQUARE 8.7.8.7.8.7.
Henry T. Smart, 1813-1879

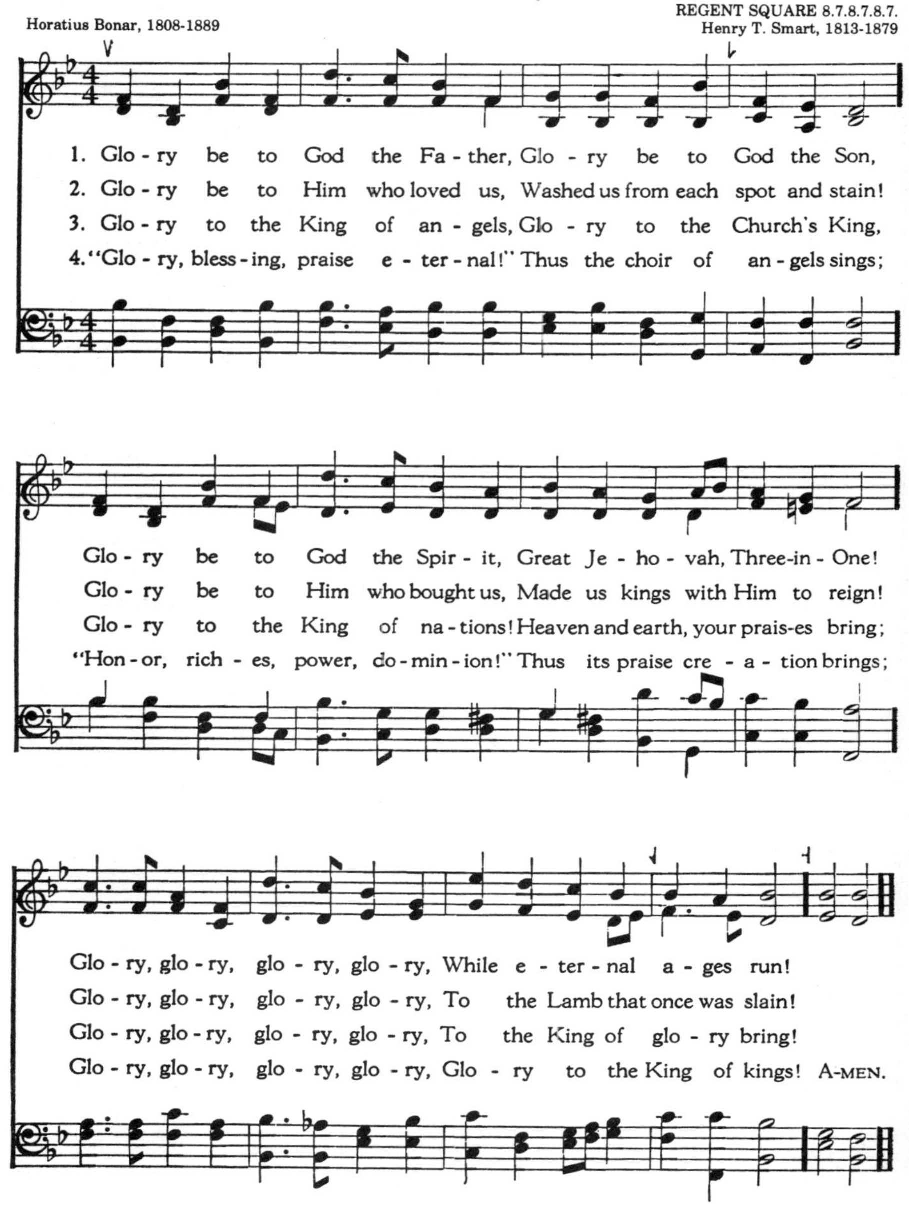

1. Glo-ry be to God the Fa-ther, Glo-ry be to God the Son,
2. Glo-ry be to Him who loved us, Washed us from each spot and stain!
3. Glo-ry to the King of an-gels, Glo-ry to the Church's King,
4. "Glo-ry, bless-ing, praise e-ter-nal!" Thus the choir of an-gels sings;
Glo-ry be to God the Spir-it, Great Je-ho-vah, Three-in-One!
Glo-ry be to Him who bought us, Made us kings with Him to reign!
Glo-ry to the King of na-tions! Heaven and earth, your prais-es bring;
"Hon-or, rich-es, power, do-min-ion!" Thus its praise cre-a-tion brings;
Glo-ry, glo-ry, glo-ry, glo-ry, While e-ter-nal a-ges run!
Glo-ry, glo-ry, glo-ry, glo-ry, To the Lamb that once was slain!
Glo-ry, glo-ry, glo-ry, glo-ry, To the King of glo-ry bring!
Glo-ry, glo-ry, glo-ry, glo-ry, Glo-ry to the King of kings! A-MEN.

O Worship the King

. . . I will sing praise to my God . . . Psa. 104:33

Robert Grant, circa 1779-1838

LYONS 10.10.11.11.
Adapted from Johann M. Haydn, 1737-1806

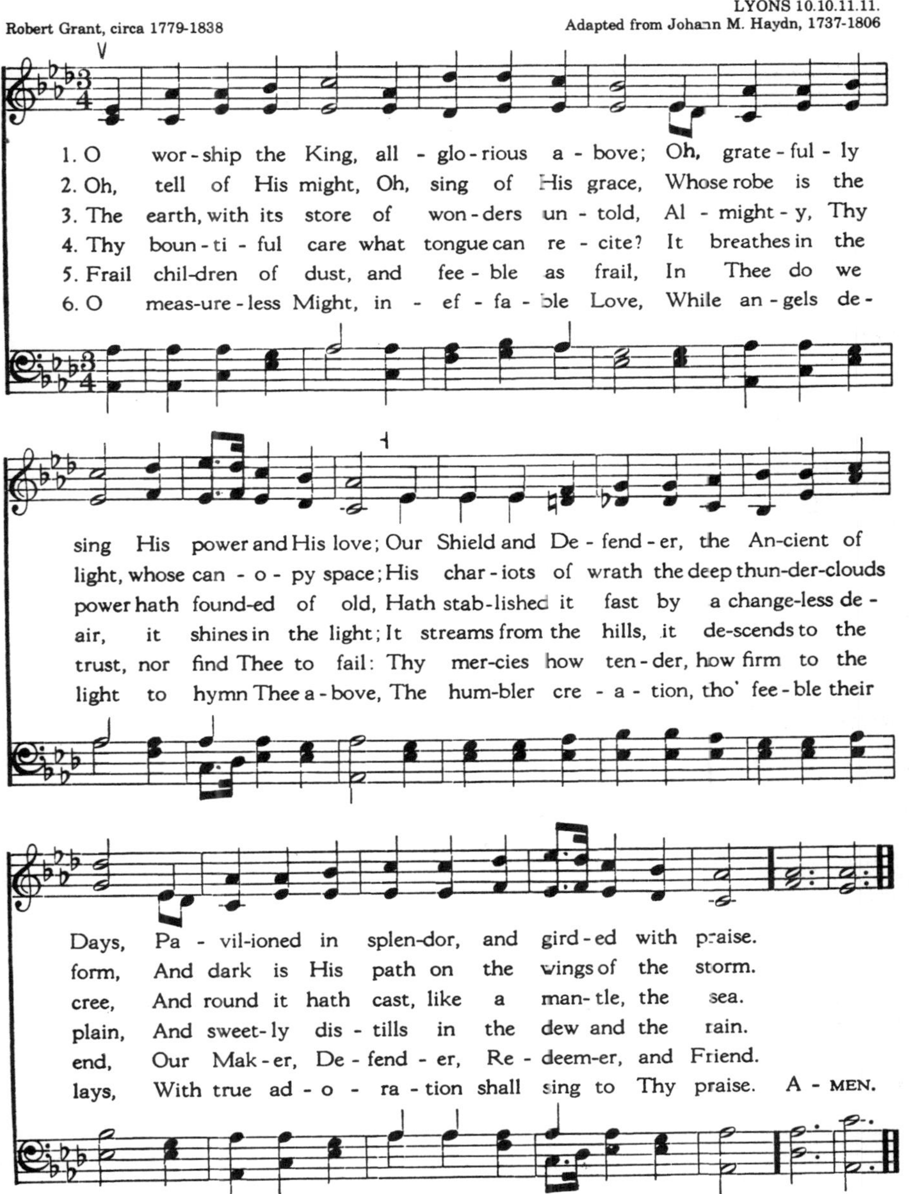

1. O wor-ship the King, all - glo-rious a - bove; Oh, grate-ful-ly
2. Oh, tell of His might, Oh, sing of His grace, Whose robe is the
3. The earth, with its store of won-ders un - told, Al - might-y, Thy
4. Thy boun-ti - ful care what tongue can re - cite? It breathes in the
5. Frail chil-dren of dust, and fee - ble as frail, In Thee do we
6. O meas-ure - less Might, in - ef - fa - ble Love, While an - gels de-

sing His power and His love; Our Shield and De - fend - er, the An-cient of
light, whose can - o - py space; His char - iots of wrath the deep thun-der-clouds
power hath found-ed of old, Hath stab-lished it fast by a change-less de -
air, it shines in the light; It streams from the hills, it de-scends to the
trust, nor find Thee to fail: Thy mer-cies how ten-der, how firm to the
light to hymn Thee a-bove, The hum-bler cre - a - tion, tho' fee-ble their

Days, Pa - vil-ioned in splen-dor, and gird-ed with praise.
form, And dark is His path on the wings of the storm.
cree, And round it hath cast, like a man-tle, the sea.
plain, And sweet-ly dis - tills in the dew and the rain.
end, Our Mak-er, De - fend - er, Re - deem-er, and Friend.
lays, With true ad - o - ra - tion shall sing to Thy praise. A - MEN.

A Mighty Fortress Is Our God

4
A Mighty Fortress Is Our God
God is our refuge and strength ... Psa. 46:1
Martin Luther, 1483-1546
Translated by Frederick H. Hedge, 1805-1890
EIN' FESTE BURG 8.7.8.7.6.6.6.6.7.
From a Meistergesang by Hans Sachs, d. 1576
Adapted by Johann Walther, 1496-1570
1. A might-y for-tress is our God, A bul-wark nev-er fail - ing;
2. Did we in our own strength con-fide, Our striv-ing would be los - ing;
3. And though this world, with dev - ils filled, Should threat-en to un-do us,
4. That Word a - bove all earth - ly powers, No thanks to them, a - bid - eth;
Our help-er He, a - mid the flood Of mor-tal ills pre-vail - ing:
Were not the right Man on our side, The Man of God's own choos - ing:
We will not fear, for God hath willed His truth to tri-umph through us:
The Spir-it and the gifts are ours Thro' Him who with us sid - eth:
For still our an - cient foe Doth seek to work us woe; His craft and power are
Dost ask who that may be? Christ Je - sus, it is He, Lord Sa - ba - oth, His
The Prince of Dark -ness grim—We trem-ble not for him; His rage we can en -
Let goods and kin - dred go, This mor-tal life al - so; The bod - y they may
great, And, armed with cru - el hate, On earth is not his e - qual.
name, From age to age the same, And He must win the bat - tle.
dure, For lo, his doom is sure, One lit - tle word shall fell him.
kill: God's truth a - bid - eth still, His king-dom is for - ev - er.

All for Jesus

5

... bringing into captivity every thought to the obedience of Christ. 2 Cor. 10:5

CONSTANCY 8.7.8.7. with Refrain
Anonymous

Mary D. James, 1810-1883

1. All for Je-sus, all for Je-sus! All my be-ing's ran-somed powers,
2. Let my hands per-form His bid-ding, Let my feet run in His ways,
3. Since my eyes were fixed on Je-sus, I've lost sight of all be-side,
4. Oh, what won-der! How a-maz-ing! Je-sus, glo-rious King of kings,

All my thoughts and words and do-ings, All my days and all my hours.
Let my eyes see Je-sus on-ly, Let my lips speak forth His praise.
So en-chained my spir-it's vi-sion, Look-ing at the Cru-ci-fied.
Deigns to call me His be-lov-ed, Lets me rest be-neath His wings.

REFRAIN

All for Je-sus, all for Je-sus! All my days and all my hours;
All for Je-sus, all for Je-sus! Let my lips speak forth His praise;
All for Je-sus, all for Je-sus! Look-ing at the Cru-ci-fied;
All for Je-sus, all for Je-sus! Rest-ing now be-neath His wings;

All for Je-sus, all for Je-sus! All my days and all my hours.
All for Je-sus, all for Je-sus! Let my lips speak forth His praise.
All for Je-sus, all for Je-sus! Look-ing at the Cru-ci-fied.
All for Je-sus, all for Je-sus! Rest-ing now be-neath His wings.

To God Be the Glory

Give unto the Lord the glory due unto his name . . . Psa. 29:2

Fanny J. Crosby, 1820-1915

TO GOD BE THE GLORY 11.11.11.11. with Refrain
William H. Doane, 1832-1915

1. To God be the glo-ry, great things He hath done, So loved He the world that He
2. O per - fect re-demp-tion, the pur-chase of blood, To ev-ery be-liev-er the
3. Great things He hath taught us, great things He hath done, And great our re-joic-ing thro'

gave us His Son, Who yield-ed His life an a-tone-ment for sin, And o-pened the
prom-ise of God; The vil - est of-fen-der who tru - ly believes, That moment from
Je - sus the Son; But pur - er, and high-er, and great-er will be Our won-der, our

REFRAIN

life - gate that all may go in.
Je - sus a par-don receives. Praise the Lord, praise the Lord, Let the earth hear His
trans-port, when Je-sus we see.

voice! Praise the Lord, praise the Lord, Let the peo-ple re-joice! O come to the

Fa-ther thro' Je - sus the Son, And give Him the glo - ry; great things He hath done.

How Great Thou Art

Great is the Lord, and greatly to be praised ... Psa. 48:1

Stuart K. Hine, b. 1899

1. O Lord, my God! When I in awe-some won-der Con-sid-er
2. When through the woods and for-est glades I wan-der And hear the
3. And when I think that God, His Son not spar-ing, Sent Him to
4. When Christ shall come with shout of ac-cla-ma-tion And take me
all the worlds Thy hands have made, I see the stars, I hear the roll-ing
birds sing sweet-ly in the trees; When I look down from loft-y moun-tain
die, I scarce can take it in; That on the cross, my bur-den glad-ly
home, what joys shall fill my heart! Then I shall bow in hum-ble ad-o-
thun-der, Thy power through-out the u-ni-verse dis-played.
gran-deur And hear the brook and feel the gen-tle breeze.
bear-ing, He bled and died to take a-way my sin.
ra-tion And there pro-claim, my God, how great Thou art!
REFRAIN
Then sings my
soul, my Sav-iour God, to Thee. How great Thou art, how great Thou art! Then
sings my soul, my Sav-iour God, to Thee. How great Thou art, how great Thou art!

Blessed Be the Name

... the Lord gave, ... blessed be the name of the Lord. Job 1:21

BLESSED BE THE NAME C.M. with Refrain
Anonymous

William H. Clark, 19th century
Refrain by Ralph E. Hudson, 1843-1901

Arranged by Ralph E. Hudson, 1843-1901
and William J. Kirkpatrick, 1838-1921

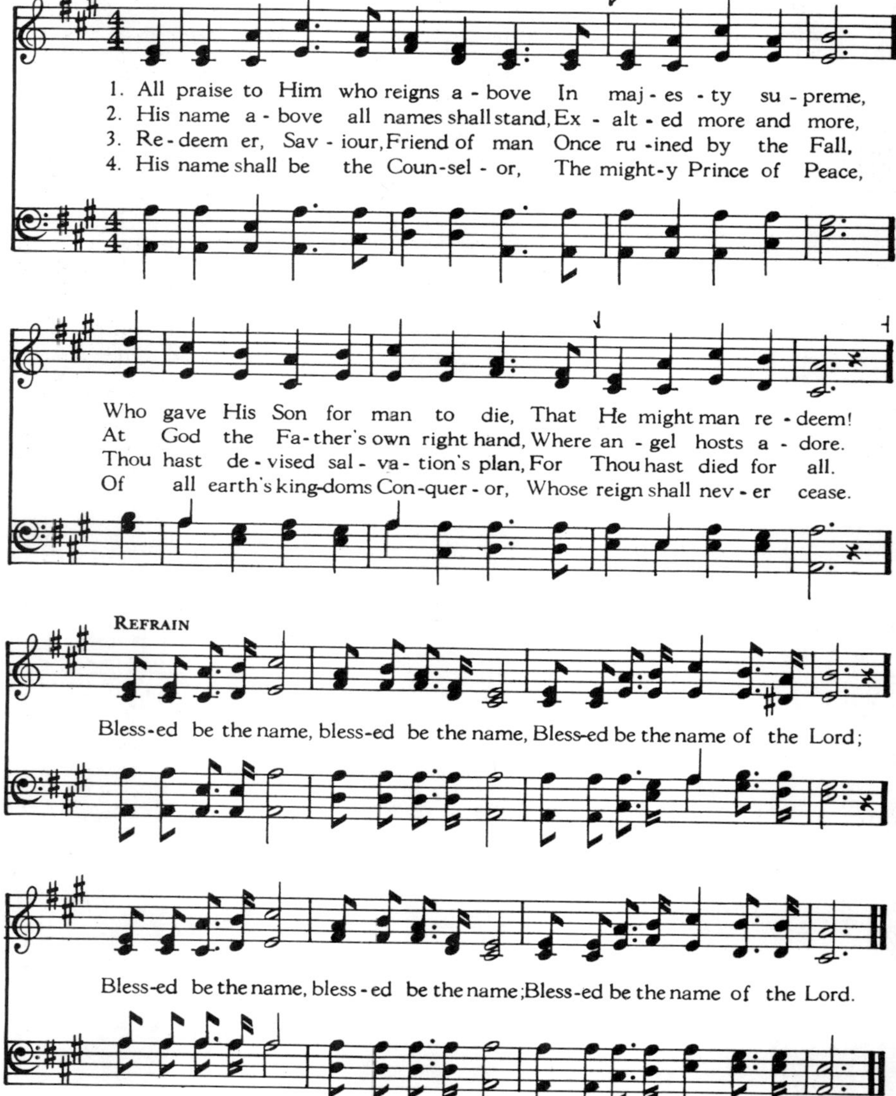

1. All praise to Him who reigns a-bove In maj-es-ty su-preme,
2. His name a-bove all names shall stand, Ex-alt-ed more and more,
3. Re-deem-er, Sav-iour, Friend of man Once ru-ined by the Fall,
4. His name shall be the Coun-sel-or, The might-y Prince of Peace,
Who gave His Son for man to die, That He might man re-deem!
At God the Fa-ther's own right hand, Where an-gel hosts a-dore.
Thou hast de-vised sal-va-tion's plan, For Thou hast died for all.
Of all earth's king-doms Con-quer-or, Whose reign shall nev-er cease.
REFRAIN
Bless-ed be the name, bless-ed be the name, Bless-ed be the name of the Lord;
Bless-ed be the name, bless-ed be the name; Bless-ed be the name of the Lord.

Oh, for a Thousand Tongues

(SECOND TUNE)

9

AZMON C.M.
Carl G. Gläser, 1784-1829
Adapted by Lowell Mason, 1792-1872

Charles Wesley, 1707-1788

1. Oh, for a thou-sand tongues to sing My great Re-deem-er's praise,
2. My gra-cious Mas-ter and my God, As-sist me to pro-claim,
3. Je-sus! the Name that charms our fears, That bids our sor-rows cease:
4. He breaks the power of can-celed sin, He sets the pris-oner free;
5. Glo-ry to God, and praise, and love Be ev-er, ev-er given
The glo-ries of my God and King, The tri-umphs of His grace!
To spread through all the earth a-broad, The hon-ors of Thy name.
'Tis mu-sic in the sin-ner's ears, 'Tis life and health and peace.
His blood can make the foul-est clean, His blood a-vailed for me.
By saints be-low and saints a-bove, The Church in earth and heaven.

Oh, for a Heart to Praise My God

10

I will praise thee, O Lord, with my whole heart . . . Psa. 9:1

AZMON C.M.
Carl G. Gläser, 1784-1829
Adapted by Lowell Mason, 1792-1872

Charles Wesley, 1707-1788

1. Oh, for a heart to praise my God, A heart from sin set free,
2. A heart re-signed, sub-mis-sive, meek, My great Re-deem-er's throne;
3. A heart in ev-ery thought re-newed, And full of love di-vine;
4. Thy na-ture, gra-cious Lord, im-part; Come quick-ly from a-bove,
A heart that al-ways feels Thy blood So free-ly shed for me!
Where on-ly Christ is heard to speak, Where Je-sus reigns a-lone.
Per-fect, and right, and pure, and good, A cop-y, Lord, of Thine!
Write Thy new name up-on my heart, Thy new, best name of Love. A-MEN.

One Day!

. . . unto them that look for him shall he appear the second time . . . Heb. 9:28

J. Wilbur Chapman, 1859-1918

CHAPMAN 11.10.11.10. with Refrain
Charles H. Marsh, 1886-1956

1. One day when heav-en was filled with His prais-es, One day when
2. One day they led Him up Cal-va-ry's moun-tain, One day they
3. One day they left Him a-lone in the gar-den, One day He
4. One day the grave could con-ceal Him no long-er, One day the
5. One day the trum-pet will sound for His com-ing, One day the

sin was as black as could be, Je-sus came forth to be
nailed Him to die on the tree; Suf-fer-ing an-guish, de-
rest-ed, from suf-fer-ing free; An-gels came down o'er His
stone rolled a-way from the door; Then He a-rose, o-ver
skies with His glo-ry will shine; Won-der-ful day, my be-

born of a Vir-gin, Dwelt a-mong men, my ex-am-ple is He!
spised and re-ject-ed, Bear-ing our sins, my Re-deem-er is He!
tomb to keep vig-il; Hope of the hope-less, my Sav-iour is He!
death He has con-quered; Now is as-cend-ed, my Lord ev-er-more!
lov-ed ones bring-ing; Glo-ri-ous Sav-iour, this Je-sus is mine!

REFRAIN
Liv-ing, He loved me; dy-ing, He saved me; Bur-ied, He

One Day!
car - ried my sins far a - way; Ris - ing, He jus - ti - fied
free - ly for - ev - er: One day He's com - ing— oh, glo - ri - ous day!

Jesus, the Very Thought of Thee

12

. . . yet believing, ye rejoice with joy unspeakable . . . 1 Pet. 1:8

From *Jesu dulcis memoria*, circa 1150
Translated by Edward Caswall, 1814-1878

ST. AGNES C.M.
John B. Dykes, 1823-1876

1. Je - sus, the ver - y thought of Thee With sweet-ness fills my breast;
2. Nor voice can sing, nor heart can frame, Nor can the mem - ory find
3. O hope of ev - ery con - trite heart, O joy of all the meek,
4. But what to those who find? Ah, this Nor tongue nor pen can show:
5. Je - sus, our on - ly joy be Thou, As Thou our prize wilt be;

But sweet - er far Thy face to see, And in Thy pres - ence rest.
A sweet - er sound than Thy blest name, O Sav - iour of man - kind!
To those who fall, how kind Thou art! How good to those who seek!
The love of Je - sus, what it is None but His loved ones know.
Je - sus, be Thou our glo - ry now, And through e - ter - ni - ty. A-MEN.

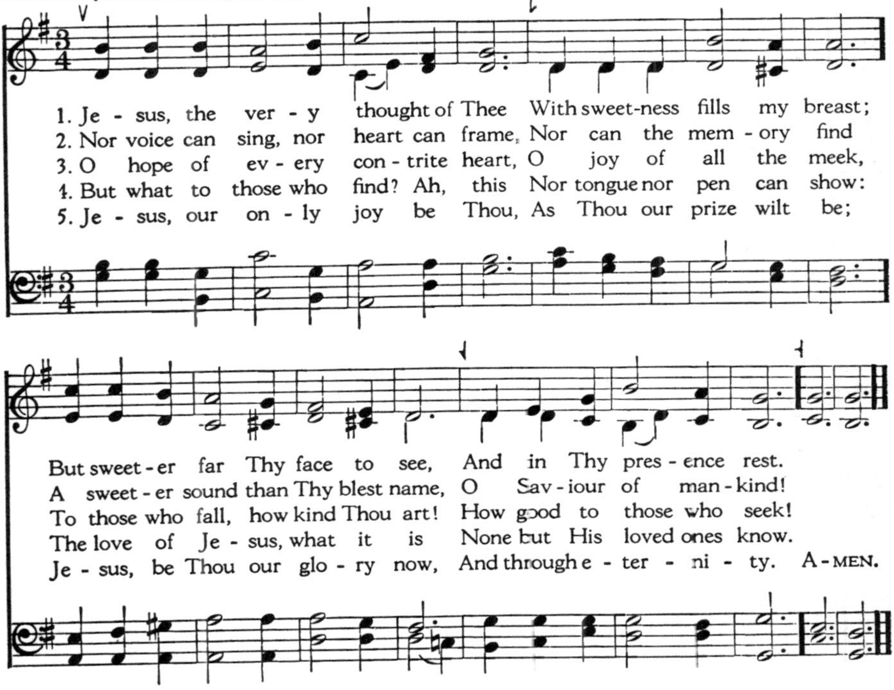

I Will Praise Him

Whoso offereth praise glorifieth me ... Psa. 50:23

I WILL PRAISE HIM 8.7.8.7. with Refrain
Margaret J. Harris, 19th century
Margaret J. Harris, 19th century

1. When I saw the cleans-ing foun-tain O - pen wide for all my sin,
2. Tho' the way seemed straight and nar-row, All I claimed was swept a - way;
3. Then God's fire up - on the al - tar Of my heart was set a - flame.
4. Bless- ed be the name of Je - sus! I'm so glad He took me in.
I o-beyed the Spir-it's woo-ing When He said, "Wilt thou be clean?"
My am - bi -tions, plans, and wish - es At my feet in ash - es lay.
I shall nev - er cease to praise Him. Glo - ry, glo - ry to His name!
He's for-giv - en my trans-gres-sions; He has cleansed my heart from sin.
REFRAIN
I will praise Him! I will praise Him! Praise the Lamb for sin-ners slain!
Give Him glo - ry, all ye peo - ple, For His blood can wash a-way each stain.

Lead Me to Calvary

... consider him that endured such contradiction of sinners ... Heb. 12:3

Jennie E. Hussey, 1874-1958

DUNCANNON C.M. with Refrain
William J. Kirkpatrick, 1838-1921

1. King of my life, I crown Thee now, Thine shall the glo - ry be;
2. Show me the tomb where Thou wast laid. Ten - der - ly mourned and wept;
3. Let me, like Ma - ry, through the gloom, Come with a gift to Thee;
4. May I be will - ing, Lord, to bear Dai - ly my cross for Thee;

Lest I for-get Thy thorn-crowned brow, Lead me to Cal - va - ry.
An - gels in robes of light ar - rayed Guard-ed Thee whilst Thou slept.
Show to me now the emp - ty tomb, Lead me to Cal - va - ry.
E - ven Thy cup of grief to share, Thou hast borne all for me.

REFRAIN
Lest I for-get Geth-sem - a - ne; Lest I for-get Thine ag - o - ny;

Lest I for-get Thy love for me, Lead me to Cal - va - ry.

1. Be-neath the cross of Je-sus I fain would take my stand—
2. Up-on that cross of Je-sus Mine eye at times can see
3. I take, O cross, thy shad-ow For my a-bid-ing place;

The shad-ow of a might-y Rock With-in a wea-ry land;
The ver-y dy-ing form of One Who suf-fered there for me;
I ask no oth-er sun-shine than The sun-shine of His face;

A home with-in the wil-der-ness, A rest up-on the way,
And from my smit-ten heart with tears Two won-ders I con-fess—
Con-tent to let the world go by, To know no gain nor loss,

From the burn-ing of the noon-tide heat, And the bur-den of the day.
The won-ders of re-deem-ing love And my un-wor-thi-ness.
My sin-ful self my on-ly shame, My glo-ry all the cross. A-MEN.

15 Beneath the Cross of Jesus

. . . the shadow of a great rock in a weary land. Isa. 32:2

Elizabeth C. Clephane, 1830-1869

ST. CHRISTOPHER 7.6.8.6.8.6.8.6.
Frederick C. Maker, 1844-1927

At the Cross

... having made peace through the blood of his cross ... Col. 1 20

Isaac Watts, 1674-1748
Refrain by Ralph E. Hudson, 1843-1901

HUDSON C.M. with Refrain
Ralph E. Hudson, 1843-1901

1. A - las! and did my Sav - iour bleed? And did my Sov-ereign die?
2. Was it for crimes that I have done He groaned up - on the tree?
3. Well might the sun in dark - ness hide And shut His glo - ries in,
4. But drops of grief can ne'er re - pay The debt of love I owe:
Would He de - vote that sa - cred head For such a worm as I?
A - maz - ing pit - y! grace un-known! And love be - yond de - gree!
When Christ, the might - y Mak - er, died For man, the crea-ture's sin.
Here, Lord, I give my - self to Thee; 'Tis all that I can do!
REFRAIN
At the cross, at the cross where I first saw the light, And the
bur - den of my heart rolled a - way, It was there by faith
I re - ceived my sight, And now I am hap - py all the day!

There Is a Fountain

. . . there shall be a fountain . . . for sin and for uncleanness. Zech. 13:1

CLEANSING FOUNTAIN C.M. with repeats
American melody
Arranged by Lowell Mason, 1792-1872

William Cowper, 1731-1800

1. There is a foun-tain filled with blood Drawn from Em-man-uel's veins;
2. The dy-ing thief re-joiced to see That foun-tain in his day;
3. Dear dy-ing Lamb, Thy pre-cious blood Shall nev-er lose its power,
4. E'er since by faith I saw the stream Thy flow-ing wounds sup-ply,
5. When this poor lisp-ing, stam-mering tongue Lies si-lent in the grave,

And sin-ners plunged be-neath that flood, Lose all their guilt-y stains:
And there may I, though vile as he, Wash all my sins a-way:
Till all the ran-somed Church of God Be saved, to sin no more:
Re-deem-ing love has been my theme, And shall be till I die:
Then in a no-bler, sweet-er song I'll sing Thy power to save:

Lose all their guilt-y stains, Lose all their guilt-y stains;
Wash all my sins a-way, Wash all my sins a-way;
Be saved, to sin no more, Be saved, to sin no more;
And shall be till I die, And shall be till I die;
I'll sing Thy power to save, I'll sing Thy power to save;

And sin-ners plunged be-neath that flood, Lose all their guilt-y stains.
And there may I, though vile as he, Wash all my sins a-way.
Till all the ran-somed Church of God Be saved, to sin no more.
Re-deem-ing love has been my theme, And shall be till I die.
Then in a no-bler, sweet-er song I'll sing Thy power to save.

Christ the Lord Is Risen Today

. . . now is Christ risen from the dead . . . 1 Cor. 15:20

EASTER HYMN 7.4.7.4.D.
Lyra Davidica, 1708
From *Compleat Psalmodist*, 1749 (altered)

Charles Wesley, 1707-1788

1. "Christ the Lord is risen to - day," Al - - - le - lu - ia!
2. Love's re - deem - ing work is done, Al - - - le - lu - ia!
3. Lives a - gain our glo - rious King; Al - - - le - lu - ia!
4. Soar we now where Christ has led, Al - - - le - lu - ia!

Sons of men and an - gels say. Al - - - le - lu - ia!
Fought the fight, the bat - tle won; Al - - - le - lu - ia!
Where, O death, is now thy sting? Al - - - le - lu - ia!
Fol - lowing our ex - alt - ed Head; Al - - - le - lu - ia!

Raise your joys and tri - umphs high; Al - - - le - lu - ia!
Death in vain for - bids Him rise, Al - - - le - lu - ia!
Dy - ing once, He all doth save: Al - - - le - lu - ia!
Made like Him, like Him we rise; Al - - - le - lu - ia!

Sing, ye heavens, and earth re - ply: Al - - - le - lu - ia!
Christ has o - pened Par - a - dise. Al - - - le - lu - ia!
Where's thy vic - to - ry, O grave? Al - - - le - lu - ia!
Ours the cross, the grave, the skies. Al - - - le - lu - ia! A-MEN.

And Can It Be That I Should Gain

... while we were yet sinners, Christ died for us. Rom. 5:8

Charles Wesley, 1707-1788

SAGINA 8.8.8.8.8.8. with Refrain
Thomas Campbell, 1777-1844

1. And can it be that I should gain An interest in the
2. 'Tis mys-tery all! Th' Im-mor-tal dies! Who can ex-plore His
3. He left His Fa-ther's throne a-bove, So free, so in-fi-
4. Long my im-pris-oned spir-it lay Fast-bound in sin and
5. No con-dem-na-tion now I dread; Je-sus, and all in

Sav-iour's blood? Died He for me, who caused His pain, For me, who
strange de-sign? In vain the first-born ser-aph tries To sound the
nite His grace; Emp-tied Him-self of all but love, And bled for
na-ture's night; Thine eye dif-fused a quick-ening ray. I woke, the
Him, is mine! A-live in Him, my liv-ing Head, And clothed in

Him to death pur-sued? A-maz-ing love! How can it be That
depths of love di-vine! 'Tis mer-cy all! Let earth a-dore; Let
A-dam's help-less race. 'Tis mer-cy all, im-mense and free! For,
dun-geon flamed with light; My chains fell off, my heart was free; I
right-eous-ness di-vine, Bold I ap-proach th' e-ter-nal throne, And

REFRAIN

Thou, my God, shouldst die for me?
an-gel minds in-quire no more.
O my God, it found out me. A-maz-ing love! How
rose, went forth, and fol-lowed Thee.
claim the crown through Christ, my own. A-maz-ing love!

And Can It Be That I Should Gain

can it be That Thou, my God, shouldst die for me! A-MEN.
How can it be That Thou, my God, shouldst die for me!

When Morning Gilds the Skies

20

. . . in the morning will I direct my prayer unto thee . . . Psa. 5:3

German, 19th century
Translated by Edward Caswall, 1814-1878

LAUDES DOMINI 6.6.6.D.
Joseph Barnby, 1838-1896

1. When morn - ing gilds the skies, My heart a - wak - ing cries,
2. To Thee, O God a - bove, I cry with glow - ing love,
3. Does sad - ness fill my mind, A so - lace here I find;
4. Be this, while life is mine, My can - ti - cle di - vine;

May Je - sus Christ be praised: A - like at work and prayer,
May Je - sus Christ be praised: This song of sa - cred joy,
May Je - sus Christ be praised: Or fades my earth - ly bliss,
May Je - sus Christ be praised: Be this th' e - ter - nal song,

To Je - sus I re - pair; May Je - sus Christ be praised.
It nev - er seems to cloy; May Je - sus Christ be praised.
My com - fort still is this: May Je - sus Christ be praised.
Through all the a - ges long: May Je - sus Christ be praised.

Worthy Is the Lamb

. . . that was slain to receive . . . honour, and glory, and blessing. Rev. 5:12

Johnson Oatman, Jr., 1856-1926

George C. Hugg, 1848-1907

1. "Wor-thy is the Lamb," the hosts of heav-en sing, As be-fore the
2. Wor-thy is the Lamb, who shed His pre-cious blood To re-store a
3. Wor-thy is the Lamb, the bleed-ing sac-ri-fice, Who for A-dam's
4. "Wor-thy is the Lamb," let men and an-gels sing; "Wor-thy is the

throne they make His prais-es ring; "Wor-thy is the Lamb the
world to hap-pi-ness and God; When no eye could pit-y
race paid such a fear-ful price; Wor-thy is the Lamb, the
Lamb," let hal-le-lu-jahs ring; And when life is past, up-

book to o-pen wide; Wor-thy is the Lamb who once was cru-ci-fied."
and no arm could save, Je-sus, for our ran-som, Him-self free-ly gave.
pas-chal Lamb of God, For the world re-ceived re-demp-tion through His blood.
on the gold-en shore, "Wor-thy is the Lamb," we'll shout for-ev-er-more.

REFRAIN
Oh, this bleed-ing Lamb, oh, this bleed-ing Lamb, Oh, this dy-ing

Lamb, He was found wor-thy; Oh, this bleed-ing Lamb, oh, this

Worthy Is the Lamb
bleed-ing Lamb, Oh, this dy-ing Lamb, He was found wor-thy!

Majestic Sweetness Sits Enthroned

22

. . . we see Jesus, . . . crowned with glory and honour . . . Heb. 2 9

OPTONVILLE C.M. with repeat
Melody by Thomas Hastings, 1784-1872
Harmony by J. Buchanan MacMillan, b. 1915

Samuel Stennett, 1727-1795

1. Ma - jes - tic sweet - ness sits en - throned Up - on the
2. No mor - tal can with Him com - pare A - mong the
3. To Him I owe my life and breath, And all the
4. To heaven, the place of His a - bode, He brings my
5. Since from His boun - ty I re - ceive Such proofs of

Sav - iour's brow; His head with ra - diant glo - ries crowned, His
sons of men; Fair - er is He than all the fair That
joys I have; He makes me tri - umph o - ver death, And
wea - ry feet; Shows me the glo - ries of my God, And
love di - vine; Had I a thou - sand hearts to give, Lord,

lips with grace o'er - flow, His lips with grace o'er - flow.
fill the heaven - ly train, That fill the heaven - ly train.
saves me from the grave, And saves me from the grave.
makes my joys com - plete, And makes my joys com - plete.
they should all be Thine, Lord, they should all be Thine.

23   All Hail the Power of Jesus' Name

(FIRST TUNE)

...God ... exalted him, and given him a name which is above every name. Phil. 2:9

Edward Perronet, 1726-1792
Stanza 4 by John Rippon, 1751-1836

DIADEM 8.6.6.8. with repeats
James Ellor, 1819-1899

1. All hail the power of Je - sus' name! Let an - gels pros-trate
2. Ye cho - sen seed of Is - rael's race, Ye ran-somed from the
3. Let ev - ery kin - dred, ev - ery tribe, On this ter - res-trial
4. Oh, that with yon - der sa - cred throng We at His feet may
fall, Let an - gels pros - trate fall; Bring forth the roy - al
fall, Ye ran - somed from the fall, Hail Him who saves you
ball, On this ter - res - trial ball, To Him all maj - es -
fall, We at His feet may fall! We'll join the ev - er -
And crown.. Him,
di - a - dem,
by His grace, And crown Him, crown Him, crown Him, crown Him, And
ty as - cribe,
last - ing song, And crown.. Him,
And crown Him, crown Him, crown Him, crown......
crown Him, crown Him, crown Him,
crown Him Lord of all, crown Him, And crown Him Lord of all!
crown Him, crown............ Him,
....Him, And crown Him Lord of all!

Crown Him with Many Crowns

... on his head were many crowns ... Rev. 19:12

DIADEMATA S.M.D.
George J. Elvey, 1816-1893
Matthew Bridges, 1800-1894

24

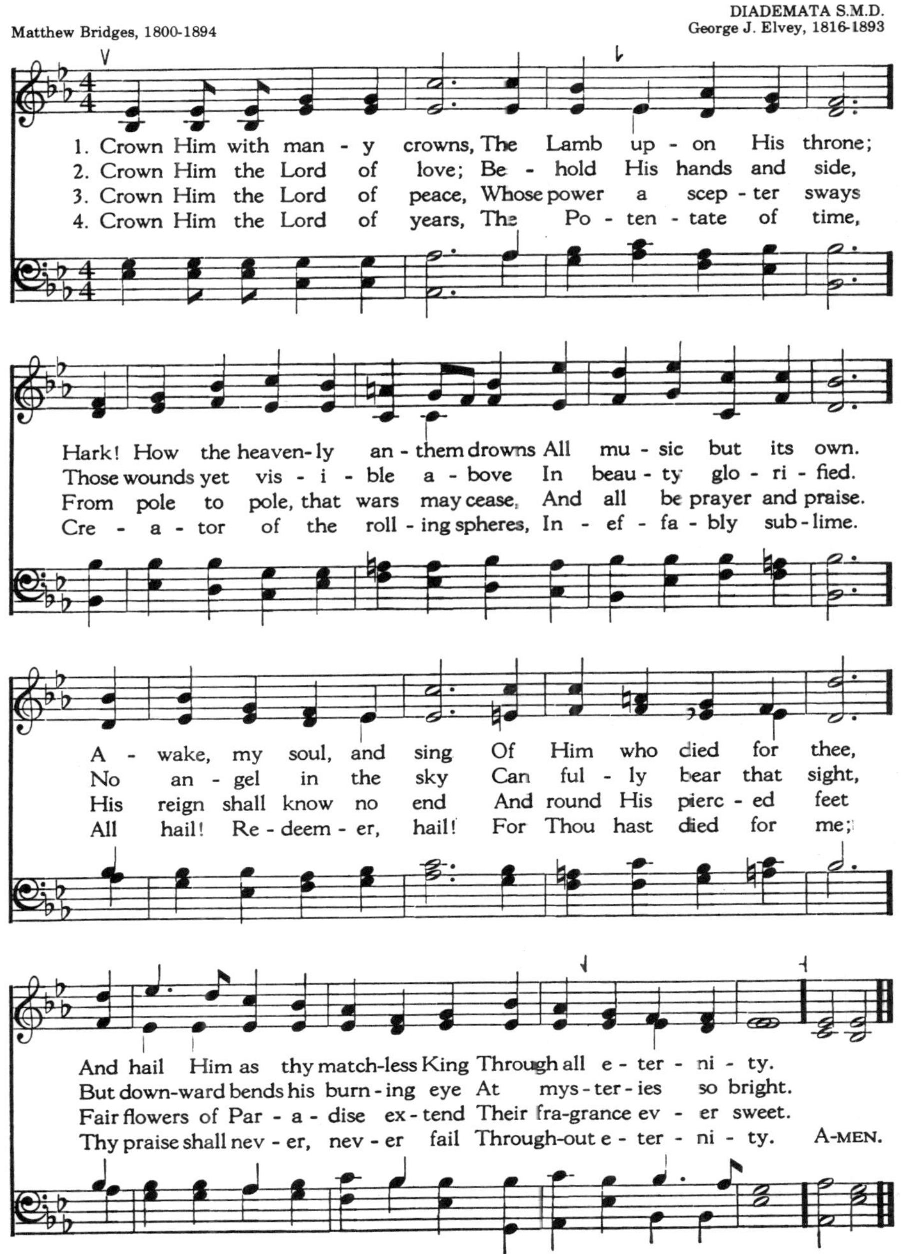

1. Crown Him with man - y crowns, The Lamb up - on His throne;
2. Crown Him the Lord of love; Be - hold His hands and side,
3. Crown Him the Lord of peace, Whose power a scep - ter sways
4. Crown Him the Lord of years, The Po - ten - tate of time,

Hark! How the heaven-ly an - them drowns All mu - sic but its own.
Those wounds yet vis - i - ble a - bove In beau - ty glo - ri - fied.
From pole to pole, that wars may cease, And all be prayer and praise.
Cre - a - tor of the roll - ing spheres, In - ef - fa - bly sub - lime.

A - wake, my soul, and sing Of Him who died for thee,
No an - gel in the sky Can ful - ly bear that sight,
His reign shall know no end And round His pierc - ed feet
All hail! Re - deem - er, hail! For Thou hast died for me;

And hail Him as thy match-less King Through all e - ter - ni - ty.
But down-ward bends his burn - ing eye At mys - ter - ies so bright.
Fair flowers of Par - a - dise ex - tend Their fra-grance ev - er sweet.
Thy praise shall nev - er, nev - er fail Through-out e - ter - ni - ty. A-MEN.

Yesterday, Today, Forever

Jesus Christ the same yesterday, and today, and forever. Heb. 13:8

Albert B. Simpson, 1843-1919

J.H. Burke, 19th century

1. Oh, how sweet the glo-rious mes-sage Sim-ple faith may claim;
2. He, who was the friend of sin-ners, Seeks thee, lost one, now;
3. Oft on earth He healed the suf-ferer By His might-y hand;
4. As of old He walked t'Em-ma-us, With them to a-bide;

Yes-ter-day, to-day, for-ev-er, Je-sus is the same.
Sin-ner, come, and at His foot-stool Pen-i-tent-ly bow.
Still our sick-ness-es and sor-rows Go at His com-mand.
So, through all life's way He walk-eth, Ev-er near our side.

Still He loves to save the sin-ful, Heal the sick and lame,
He who said, "I'll not con-demn thee; Go and sin no more,"
He who gave His heal-ing vir-tue To a wo-man's touch,
Soon a-gain we shall be-hold Him—Has-ten, Lord, the day!

Cheer the mourn-er, still the tem-pest— Glo-ry to His name!
Speaks to thee that word of par-don As in days of yore.
To the faith that claims His full-ness Still will give as much.
But 'twill still be "this same Je-sus," As He went a-way.

REFRAIN

Yes-ter-day, to-day, for-ev-er, Je-sus is the same;

Yesterday, Today, Forever

All may change, but Je-sus nev - er! Glo-ry to His name!
Glo - ry to His name; Glo - ry to His name;
All may change, but Je-sus nev-er! Glo-ry to His name.

When I Survey the Wondrous Cross   26

But what things were gain to me, those I counted loss for Christ. Phil. 3:7

HAMBURG L.M.
From *Psalm Tone I*
Adapted by Lowell Mason, 1792-1872

Isaac Watts, 1674-1748

1. When I sur-vey the won-drous cross On which the Prince of glo - ry died,
2. For - bid it, Lord, that I should boast, Save in the death of Christ my God;
3. See, from His head, His hands, His feet, Sor-row and love flow min - gled down-
4. Were the whole realm of na - ture mine, That were a pres - ent far too small;

My rich-est gain I count but loss, And pour con-tempt on all my pride.
All the vain things that charm me most, I sac-ri-fice them to His blood.
Did e'er such love and sor - row meet, Or thorns com-pose so rich a crown?
Love so a-maz - ing, so di - vine, De-mands my soul, my life, my all. A-MEN.

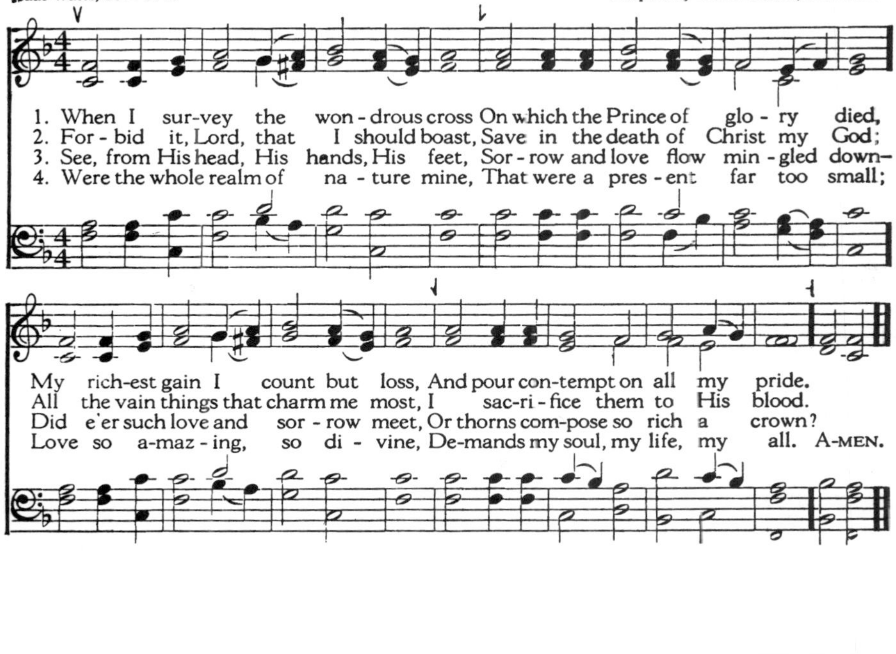

Praise Him! Praise Him!

...praise him according to his excellent greatness. Psa. 150:2

Fanny J. Crosby, 1820-1915

JOYFUL SONG Irregular with Refrain
Chester G. Allen, 1838-1878

1. Praise Him! Praise Him! Je-sus, our bless-ed Re-deem-er! Sing, O
2. Praise Him! Praise Him! Je-sus, our bless-ed Re-deem-er! For our
3. Praise Him! Praise Him! Je-sus, our bless-ed Re-deem-er! Heaven-ly

earth; His won-der-ful love pro-claim! Hail Him! Hail Him! High-est arch-
sins He suf-fered, and bled, and died; He our rock, our hope of e-
por-tals loud with ho-san-nas ring. Je-sus, Sav-iour, reign-eth for-

an-gels in glo-ry; Strength and hon-or give to His ho-ly name!
ter-nal sal-va-tion; Hail Him! Hail Him! Je-sus, the cru-ci-fied.
ev-er and ev-er; Crown Him! Crown Him! Proph-et, and Priest, and King!

Like a shep-herd Je-sus will guard His chil-dren; In His arms He
Sound His prais-es— Je-sus who bore our sor-rows; Love un-bound-ed.
Christ is com-ing, o-ver the world vic-to-rious; Power and glo-ry

REFRAIN

car-ries them all day long.
won-der-ful, deep, and strong! Praise Him! Praise Him! Tell of His
un-to the Lord be-long.

Praise Him! Praise Him!

ex - cel-lent great-ness; Praise Him! Praise Him, ev - er in joy - ful song!

Jesus Paid It All

28

. . . your sins . . . they shall be as white as snow . . . Isa. 1:18

ALL TO CHRIST 6.6.7.7. with Refrain

Elvina M. Hall, 1820-1889

John T. Grape, 1835-1915

1. I hear the Sav - iour say, "Thy strength in - deed is small;
2. Lord, now in - deed I find Thy power, and Thine a - lone,
3. For noth - ing good have I Where - by Thy grace to claim—
4. And when, be - fore the throne, I stand in Him com - plete,

Child of weak - ness, watch and pray, Find in Me thine all in all."
Can change the lep - er's spots And melt the heart of stone.
I'll wash my gar - ments white In the blood of Cal - vary's Lamb.
"Je - sus died my soul to save," My lips shall still re - peat.

REFRAIN

Je - sus paid it all, All to Him I owe;

Sin had left a crim - son stain, He washed it white as snow.

He Is Coming Again

. . . see the Son of man coming in a cloud with power and great glory. Luke 21:27

Mabel J. Camp, 1871-1937

CAMP Irregular with Refrain
Mabel J. Camp, 1871-1937

1. Lift up your heads, Pil - grims a - wea - ry; See day's ap - proach Now
2. Dark was the night, Sin warred a - gainst us; Heav - y the load Of
3. O bless - ed hope! O bliss - ful prom-ise! Fill - ing our hearts With
4. E - ven so, come, Pre-cious Lord Je - sus; Cre - a - tion waits re -

crim - son the sky; Night shad - ows flee, And your Be - lov - ed, A -
sor - row we bore; But now we see Signs of His com - ing; Our
rap - ture di - vine; O day of days! Hail Thy ap - pear-ing! Thy
demp-tion to see; Caught up in clouds, Soon we shall meet Thee; O

REFRAIN

wait - ed with long - ing, At last draw-eth nigh.
hearts glow with - in us, Joy's cup run-neth o'er! He is com-ing a -
tran - scend-ent glo - ry For - ev - er shall shine.
bless - ed as - sur-ance, For - ev - er with Thee!

gain, He is com - ing a - gain, The ver - y same Je - sus, Re -

ject - ed of men; He is com-ing a - gain, He is com-ing a - gain;

He Is Coming Again

With power and great glo - ry, He is com - ing a - gain!
is com - ing a - gain!

My Lord Will Come Some Day 30

. . . and every eye shall see him . . . Rev. 1:7

Alice S. MacMillan, b. 1900

C. Austin Miles, 1868-1946

1. When dark the night and bur - dens press, When steep and rough the way,
2. I lis - ten for His bless - ed voice, I seek to watch and pray;
3. At ear - ly dawn I watch for Him I watch for Him at noon;
4. As eve-ning shad - ows gath - er 'round And dark - en all the sky,

This hope o'er-floods my soul with joy: My Lord will come some day.
I trust His pre - cious prom - ise true, My Lord will come some day.
My heart sings o'er the sweet re - frain, "My Lord is com - ing soon."
I lift my head, I cry with joy, "His com - ing draw - eth nigh."

REFRAIN

Some day, Some day, Some day, some day, My Lord will come some day.

Through His won-drous grace I shall see His face; My Lord will come some day.

Christ Returneth

. . . ye shall see the Son of man . . . coming in the clouds of heaven. Mark 14:62

H.L. Turner, 19th century

James McGranahan, 1840-1907

1. It may be at morn, when the day is a-wak-ing, When sun-light through
2. It may be at mid - day, it may be at twi-light, It may be, per-
3. While its hosts cry ho - san - na, from heav - en de-scend-ing, With glo - ri - fied
4. O joy, O de-light, should we go with-out dy - ing! No sick-ness, no

dark - ness and shad-ow is break-ing, That Je - sus will come in the
chance, that the black-ness of mid-night Will burst in - to light in the
saints and the an - gels at - tend-ing, With grace on His brow, like a
sad - ness, no dread-ing, no cry - ing! Caught up through the clouds with our

full - ness of glo - ry To re - ceive from the world His own.
blaze of His glo - ry, When Je - sus re - ceives His own.
ha - lo of glo - ry, Will Je - sus re - ceive His own.
Lord in - to glo - ry, When Je - sus re - ceives His own.

REFRAIN

O Lord Je - sus, how long, how long Ere we shout the glad song? Christ re-

turn-eth– Hal - le - lu - jah! Hal - le - lu - jah! A - men. Hal - le - lu - jah! A - men.

Depth of Mercy! Can There Be 32

For thy mercy is great above the heavens . . . Psa. 108:4

Charles Wesley, 1707-1788

WEBER 7.7.7.7.
Adapted from Carl M. von Weber, 1786-1826

1. Depth of mer-cy! Can there be Mer-cy still re-served for me?
2. I have long with-stood His grace, Long pro-voked Him to His face,
3. Lord, in-cline me to re-pent; Let me now my fall la-ment,
4. Still for me the Sav-iour stands, Shows His wounds, and spreads His hands;

Can my God His wrath for-bear? Me, the chief of sin-ners spare?
Would not heark-en to His calls, Grieved Him by a thou-sand falls.
Deep-ly my re-volt de-plore, Weep, be-lieve, and sin no more.
God is love, I know, I feel. Je-sus weeps, and loves me still.

Oh, for a Faith That Will Not Shrink 33

. . . Lord, Increase our faith. Luke 17:5

William H. Bathurst, 1796-1877

AZMON C.M.
Melody by Carl G. Gläser, 1784-1829
Adapted by Lowell Mason, 1792-1872

1. Oh, for a faith that will not shrink, Though pressed by man-y a foe,
2. That will not mur-mur or com-plain Be-neath the chas-tening rod,
3. A faith that shines more bright and clear When tem-pests rage with-out;
4. That bears, un-moved, the world's dread frown, Nor heeds its scorn-ful smile;
5. Lord, give us such a faith as this; And then, what-e'er may come,

That will not trem-ble on the brink Of an-y earth-ly woe;
But, in the hour of grief or pain, Will lean up-on its God;
That when in dan-ger knows no fear, In dark-ness feels no doubt;
That seas of trou-ble can-not drown, Nor Sa-tan's arts be-guile.
We'll taste, e'en here, the hal-lowed bliss Of an e-ter-nal home. A-MEN.

The Comforter Has Come

. . . he shall give you another Comforter, . . . John 14:16

Frank Bottome, 1823-1894

COMFORTER 12.12.12.6. with Refrain
William J. Kirkpatrick, 1838-1921

1. Oh, spread the ti - dings 'round wher - ev - er man is found, Wher-
2. The long, long night is past, the morn - ing breaks at last, And
3. Lo, the great King of kings, with heal - ing in His wings, To
4. O bound - less love di - vine! How shall this tongue of mine To

ev - er hu-man hearts and hu - man woes a - bound; Let ev - ery Chris-tian
hushed the dread-ful wail and fu - ry of the blast, As o'er the gold-en
ev - ery cap-tive soul a full de - liv-erance brings; And through the va-cant
won-dering mor - tals tell the match-less grace di - vine—That I, a child of

tongue pro - claim the joy - ful sound: The Com - fort - er has come!
hills the day ad - vanc - es fast! The Com - fort - er has come!
cells the song of tri - umph rings; The Com - fort - er has come!
hell, should in His im - age shine! The Com - fort - er has come!

REFRAIN
The Com - fort - er has come, The Com - fort - er has come! The

Ho - ly Ghost from Heaven, The Fa-ther's prom-ise given; Oh, spread the ti - dings

The Comforter Has Come
'round wher - ev - er man is found—The Com - fort - er has come!

Old Time Power
35
. . . he shall baptize you with the Holy Ghost, and with fire. Matt. 3:11
TABERNACLE 8.7.8.7. with Refrain
Paul Rader, 1879-1938
Paul Rader, 1879-1938

1. We are gath-ered for Thy bless-ing, We will wait up - on our God;
2. We will glo - ry in Thy pow - er, We will sing of won-drous grace;
3. Bring us low in prayer be - fore Thee, And with faith our souls in - spire,

We will trust in Him who loved us, And who bought us with His blood.
In our midst, as Thou hast prom-ised, Come, oh, come, and take Thy place.
Till we claim, by faith, the prom - ise Of the Ho - ly Ghost and fire.

REFRAIN
Spir - it, now melt and move All of our hearts with love,

Breathe on us from a - bove With old - time power.

I Lay My Sins on Jesus

Who his own self bare our sins in his own body ... 1 Pet. 2:24

RUTHERFORD 7.6.7.6.D.
Chrétien Urhan, 1790-1845
Arranged by Edward F. Rimbault, 1816-1876

Horatius Bonar, 1808-1889

1. I lay my sins on Je - sus, The spot - less Lamb of God;
2. I lay my wants on Je - sus; All full - ness dwells in Him.
3. I rest my soul on Je - sus, This wea - ry soul of mine;
4. I long to be like Je - sus— Meek, lov - ing, low - ly, mild;

He bears them all, and frees us From the ac - curs - ed load.
He heals all my dis - eas - es; He doth my soul re - deem.
His right hand me em - brac - es, I on His breast re - cline.
I long to be, like Je - sus, The Fa - ther's ho - ly child.

I bring my guilt to Je - sus To wash my crim - son stains
I lay my griefs on Je - sus, My bur - dens, and my cares—
I love the name of Je - sus, Em - man - uel, Christ, the Lord;
I long to be with Je - sus A - mid the heaven - ly throng,

White in His blood most pre - cious, Till not a spot re - mains.
He from them all re - leas - es; He all my sor - rows shares.
Like fra-grance on the breez - es, His name a - broad is poured.
To sing with saints His prais - es, To learn the an - gels' song. A - MEN.

Go and Tell Them

. . . go thou and preach the kingdom of God. Luke 9:60

Albert B. Simpson, 1843-1919

Melody by Albert B. Simpson, 1843-1919
Harmony by C. Buchanan MacMillan, b. 1915

1. Send the gos-pel of sal-va-tion To a world of dy-ing men;
2. 'Tis the Church's great com-mis-sion, 'Tis the Mas-ter's last com-mand;
3. Tell it out to Chi-na's mil-lions, Tell it out in fair Ja-pan;
4. 'Mid the lone Ti-bet-an moun-tains, By the O-ri-no-co's strand,
5. Christ is gath-er-ing out a peo-ple To His name from ev-ery race;
6. Give the gos-pel as a wit-ness To a world of sin-ful men,

Tell it out to ev-ery na-tion Till the Lord shall come a-gain.
Christ has died for ev-ery crea-ture, Tell it out in ev-ery land.
Tell it by the might-y Zai-re Tell it in the dark Su-dan.
O'er the burn-ing plains of In-dia— Tell it out in ev-ery land.
Haste to give the in-vi-ta-tion Ere shall end the day of grace.
Till the Bride shall be com-plet-ed And the Lord shall come a-gain.

REFRAIN
Go and tell them, go and tell them Je-sus died for sin-ful men;

Go and tell them, go and tell them He is com-ing back a-gain.

Harmony copyright 1962 by Christian Publications, Inc.

O Boundless Salvation

. . . it is the power of God unto salvation to every one that believeth . . . Rom. 1:16

William Booth, 1829-1912

BOOTH 11.11.11.12.11.
Attributed to J. Ellis, 19th century

1. O bound-less sal - va - tion, deep o - cean of love! O full - ness of
2. My sins, they are man - y, their stains are so deep, And bit - ter the
3. The tide now is flow-ing; I'm touch-ing the wave, I hear the loud
4. And now, hal - le - lu - jah! The rest of my days Shall glad - ly be
mer - cy Christ brought from a - bove, The whole world re - deem - ing, so
tears of re - morse that I weep; But weep - ing is use - less— thou
call of "the Might-y to save." My faith's grow-ing bold - er— de-
spent in pro - mot - ing His praise, Who o - pened His bos - om to
rich and so free, Now flow - ing for all men, Now flow - ing for
great crim - son sea, Thy wa - ters can cleanse me, Thy wa - ters can
liv - ered I'll be! I plunge 'neath the wa - ters, I plunge 'neath the
pour out this sea Of bound-less sal - va - tion, Of bound-less sal -
all men, Now flow - ing for all men—Come, roll o - ver me!
cleanse me, Thy wa - ters can cleanse me—Come, roll o - ver me!
wa - ters, I plunge 'neath the wa - ters—They roll o - ver me!
va - tion, Of bound - less sal - va - tion, For you and for me!

Christ in Me

. . . Christ in you, the hope of glory. Col. 1:27

Albert B. Simpson, 1843-1919

Albert B. Simpson, 1843-1919

1. This is my won-der-ful sto-ry—Christ to my heart has come;
2. Was there e'er sto-ry so mov-ing, Sto-ry of love and pain;
3. I am so glad I re-ceived Him, Je-sus, my heart's dear King;
4. How can I ev-er be lone-ly, How can I ev-er fall;
5. Now in His bos-om con-fid-ing, This my glad song shall be:

Je-sus, the King of glo-ry, Finds in my heart a home.
Was there e'er Bride-groom so lov-ing, Seek-ing our hearts to gain?
I who so of-ten have grieved Him, All to His feet would bring.
What can I want, if on-ly Christ is my all in all?
I am in Je-sus a-bid-ing, Je-sus a-bides in me.

REFRAIN
Christ in me, Christ in me, Christ in me—Oh, won-der-ful sto-ry;

Christ in me, Christ in me, Christ in me, the hope of glo-ry.

40
Wonderful Peace
. . . we have peace with God through our Lord Jesus Christ. Rom. 5:1
W.D. Cornell, 19th century (altered)
Melody by W.G. Cooper, 19th century
1. Far a - way in the depths of my spir - it to - night Rings a
2. I am rest - ing to - night in this won - der - ful peace, Rest - ing
3. And I think when I rise to that cit - y of peace, Where the
4. O dear soul, are you here with - out com - fort and rest, March - ing
mel - o - dy sweet - er than psalm; And in heav - en - ly strains it un -
sweet - ly in Je - sus' con - trol; For I'm kept from all dan - ger by
Au - thor of peace I shall see, That one strain of the song which the
down the rough path - way of time? Make Je - sus your friend ere the
ceas - ing - ly falls O'er my soul like an in - fi - nite calm.
night and by day, And His glo - ry is flood - ing my soul!
ran - somed will sing In that heav - en - ly king - dom will be:
shad - ows grow dark; Oh, ac - cept now this peace so sub - lime!
REFRAIN
Peace, peace, won - der - ful peace, Com - ing down from the Fa - ther a - bove, Sweep
o - ver my spir - it for - ev - er, I pray, In fath - om - less bil - lows of love!

Love Divine, All Loves Excelling

41

... charity, which is the bond of perfectness. Col. 3:14

BEECHER 8.7.8.7.D.
John Zundel, 1815-1882

Charles Wesley, 1707-1788

1. Love di - vine, all loves ex - cell - ing, Joy of heaven, to earth come down;
2. Breathe, oh, breathe Thy lov - ing Spir - it In - to ev - ery trou - bled breast;
3. Come, Al - might-y, to de - liv - er, Let us all Thy life re - ceive;
4. Fin - ish, then, Thy new cre - a - tion, Pure and spot - less let us be;

Fix in us Thy hum - ble dwell - ing, All Thy faith - ful mer - cies crown.
Let us all in Thee in - her - it, Let us find the prom - ised rest;
Sud - den - ly re - turn, and nev - er, Nev - er - more Thy tem - ples leave.
Let us see Thy great sal - va - tion Per - fect - ly re-stored in Thee;

Je - sus, Thou art all com - pas - sion, Pure, un - bound-ed love Thou art—
Take a - way the love of sin - ning; Al - pha and O - me - ga be;
Thee we would be al - ways bless - ing, Serve Thee as Thy hosts a - bove,
Changed from glo - ry in - to glo - ry Till in heaven we take our place,

Vis - it us with Thy sal - va - tion, En - ter ev - ery trem-bling heart.
End of faith, as its be - gin-ning, Set our hearts at lib - er - ty.
Pray, and praise Thee with-out ceas-ing, Glo - ry in Thy per-fect love.
Till we cast our crowns be - fore Thee, Lost in won-der, love, and praise. A-MEN.

42 Since the Fullness of His Love Came In

And to know the love of Christ, which passeth knowledge . . . Eph. 3:19

Eliza E. Hewitt, 1851-1920

Bentley D. Ackley, 1872-1958

1. Once my way was dark and drear-y, For my heart was full of sin,
2. There is grace for all the low-ly, Grace to keep the trust-ing soul,
3. Let me spread a-broad the sto-ry, Oth-er souls to Je-sus win;
But the sky is bright and cheer-y, Since the full-ness of His love came in.
Power to cleanse and make me ho-ly; Je-sus shall my yield-ed life con-trol.
For the cross is now my glo-ry, Since the full-ness of His love came in.
REFRAIN
I can nev-er tell how much I love Him, I can nev-er tell His love for me;
For it pass-eth hu-man meas-ure Like a deep, un-fath-omed sea;
deep, un-fath-omed sea;
'Tis re-deem-ing love in Christ my Sav-iour, In my soul the heaven-ly joys be-gin;

Since the Fullness of His Love Came In

And I live for Je-sus on-ly, Since the full-ness of His love came in.

Fully Surrendered
43

...yield your members servants to righteousness unto holiness. Rom. 6:19

Alfred C. Snead, 1884-1961

George C. Stebbins, 1846-1945

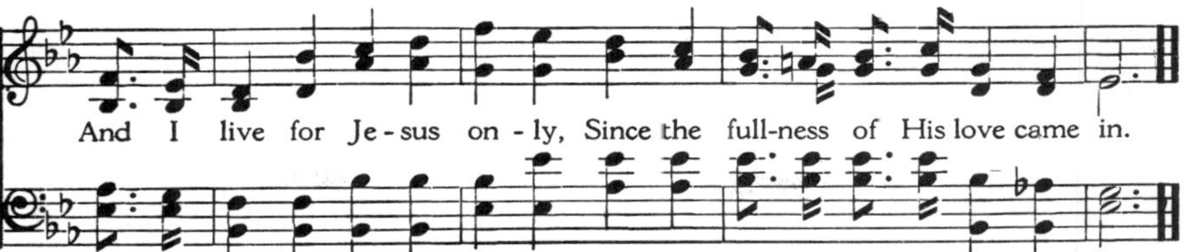

1. Ful - ly   sur-ren-dered, Lord, I would be,   Ful - ly sur - ren-dered,
2. Ful - ly   sur-ren-dered—life, time, and all,   All   Thou hast given me
3. Ful - ly   sur-ren-dered—sil - ver and gold,   His, who hath given me
4. Ful - ly   sur-ren-dered—Lord, I am Thine;   Ful - ly sur - ren-dered,

dear   Lord, to Thee.   All on the al - tar laid, Sur - ren - der
held   at Thy call.   Speak but the word to me, Glad - ly I'll
rich - es un - told.   All, all be - long to Thee, For Thou didst
Sav - iour di - vine!   Live Thou Thy life in me; All full - ness

ful - ly made, Thou hast my ran - som paid; I yield to Thee.
fol - low Thee, Now and e - ter - nal - ly O - bey my Lord.
pur - chase me, Thine ev - er - more to be, Je - sus, my Lord.
dwells in Thee; Not I, but Christ in me, Christ all in all.

My Jesus, I Love Thee

We love him, because he first loved us. 1 John 4:19

William R. Featherstone, 1846-1873

GORDON 11.11.11.11.
Adoniram J. Gordon, 1836-1895

1. My Je - sus, I love Thee, I know Thou art mine,
2. I love Thee be - cause Thou hast first lov - ed me,
3. I'll love Thee in life, I will love Thee in death,
4. In man - sions of glo - ry and end - less de - light,

For Thee all the fol - lies of sin I re - sign;
And pur - chased my par - don on Cal - va - ry's tree;
And praise Thee as long as Thou lend - est me breath;
I'll ev - er a - dore Thee in heav - en so bright;

My gra - cious Re - deem - er, my Sav - iour art Thou,
I love Thee for wear - ing the thorns on Thy brow;
And say, when the death - dew lies cold on my brow,
I'll sing with the glit - ter - ing crown on my brow,

If ev - er I loved Thee, my Je - sus, 'tis now.
If ev - er I loved Thee, my Je - sus, 'tis now.
If ev - er I loved Thee, my Je - sus, 'tis now.
If ev - er I loved Thee, my Je - sus, 'tis now.

Alleluia

Jerry Sinclair, 20th century

1. Al - le - lu - ia, al - le - lu - ia, Al - le - lu - ia, al - le - lu - ia,
Al - le - lu - ia, al - le - lu - ia, Al - le - lu - ia, al - le - lu - ia.

2. Lord, I love you,
3. I will serve Him,
4. He is coming.

Amazing Grace

And God is able to make all grace abound toward you . . . 2 Cor. 9:8

AMAZING GRACE C.M.
American melody
Carrell and Clayton's *Virginia Harmony*, 1831
Arranged by Edwin O. Excell, 1851-1921

John Newton, 1725-1807
Stanza 6 by John P. Rees, circa b. 1859

1. A - maz - ing grace, how sweet the sound That saved a wretch like me!
2. 'Twas grace that taught my heart to fear, And grace my fears re - lieved;
3. Through man - y dan - gers, toils, and snares. I have al - read - y come;
4. The Lord has prom - ised good to me, His Word my hope se - cures;
5. And when this flesh and heart shall fail, And mor - tal life shall cease;
6. When we've been there ten thou - sand years, Bright shin - ing as the sun,

I once was lost, but now am found-Was blind, but now I see.
How pre - cious did that grace ap - pear The hour I first be - lieved!
'Tis grace has brought me safe thus far, And grace will lead me home.
He will my shield and por - tion be As long as life en - dures.
I shall pos - sess with - in the veil A life of joy and peace.
We've no less days to sing God's praise Than when we first be - gun.

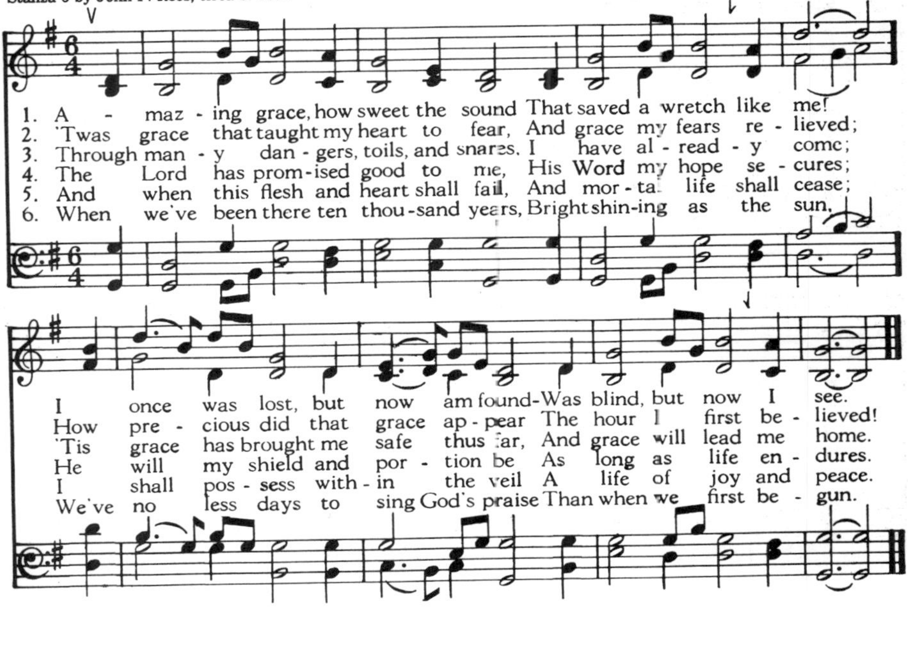

The Old Rugged Cross

. . . who for the joy . . . endured the cross, despising the shame . . . Heb. 12:2

George Bennard, 1873-1958

OLD RUGGED CROSS Irregular with Refrain
George Bennard, 1873-1958

1. On a hill far a - way stood an old rug - ged cross, The em-blem of
2. Oh, that old rug-ged cross, so de-spised by the world, Has a won-drous at -
3. In the old rug-ged cross, stained with blood so di - vine, A won - drous
4. To the old rug-ged cross I will ev - er be true, Its shame and re -
suf - fering and shame; And I love that old cross where the dear - est and best
trac - tion for me; For the dear Lamb of God left His glo - ry a - bove
beau - ty I see; For 'twas on that old cross Je - sus suf - fered and died
proach glad-ly bear; Then He'll call me some day to my home far a - way,
REFRAIN
For a world of lost sin - ners was slain.
To bear it to dark Cal - va - ry. So I'll cher - ish the old rug - ged
To par - don and sanc - ti - fy me.
Where His glo - ry for - ev - er I'll share. cross, the
cross, Till my tro - phies at last I lay down; I will cling to the
old rug-ged cross,

The Old Rugged Cross

old rug-ged cross, And ex-change it some day for a crown.
cross, the old rug-ged cross,

Almost Persuaded

48

. . . Almost thou persuadest me to be a Christian. Acts 26:28

Philip P. Bliss, 1838-1876

Philip P. Bliss, 1838-1876

1. Al - most per - suad - ed, now to be - lieve; Al - most per - suad - ed,
2. Al - most per - suad - ed, come, come to - day; Al - most per - suad - ed,
3. Al - most per - suad - ed, har - vest is past! Al - most per - suad - ed,

Christ to re - ceive; Seems now some soul to say: "Go, Spir - it,
turn not a - way; Je - sus in - vites you here, An - gels are
doom comes at last! Al - most can - not a - vail; Al - most is

go Thy way, Some more con - ven - ient day On Thee I'll call."
lin - gering near, Prayers rise from hearts so dear— O wan-derer, come.
but to fail! Sad, sad, that bit - ter wail— Al - most, but lost.

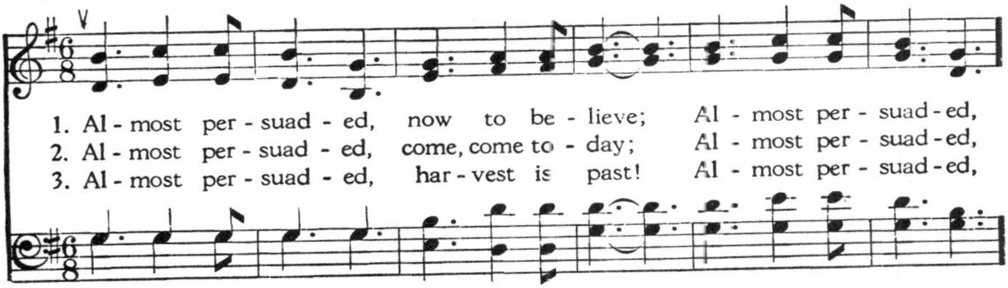

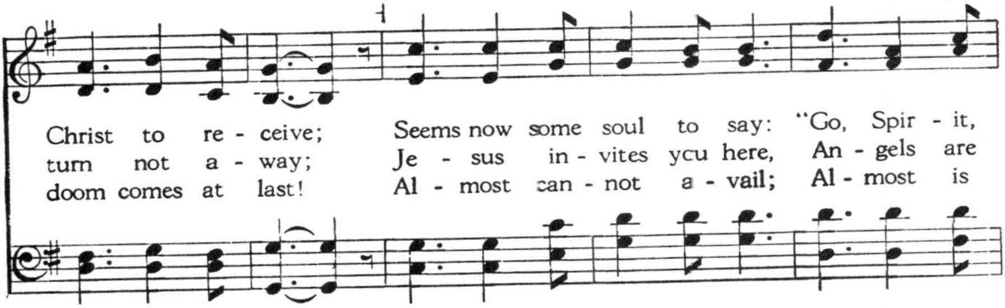

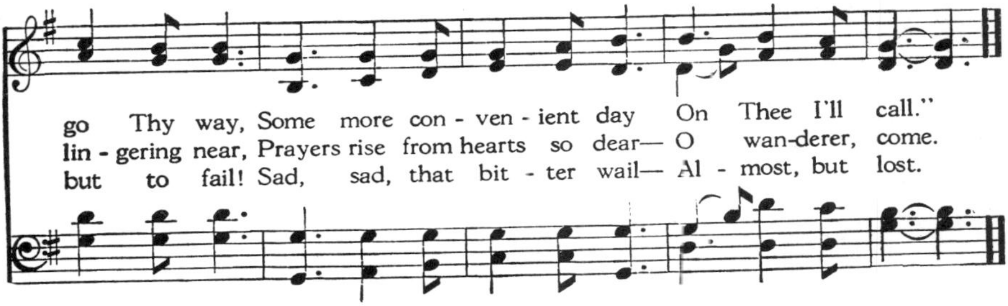

Wonderful Grace of Jesus

. . . where sin abounded, grace did much more abound. Rom. 5:20

Haldor Lillenas, 1885-1959
WONDERFUL GRACE Irregular with Refrain
Haldor Lillenas, 1885-1959

1. Won - der - ful grace of Je - sus, Great - er than all my sin—
2. Won - der - ful grace of Je - sus, Reach - ing to all the lost—
3. Won - der - ful grace of Je - sus, Reach - ing the most de - filed—

How shall my tongue des - cribe it, Where shall its praise be - gin?
By it I have been par - doned, Saved to the ut - ter - most;
By its trans-form-ing pow - er, Mak - ing him God's dear child,

Tak - ing a - way my bur - den, Set - ting my spir - it free;
Chains have been torn a - sun - der, Giv - ing me lib - er - ty;
Pur - chas - ing peace and heav - en, For all e - ter - ni - ty;

For the won - der - ful grace of Je - sus reach - es me.
For the won - der - ful grace of Je - sus reach - es me.
And the won - der - ful grace of Je - sus reach - es me.

REFRAIN

Won-der - ful the match-less grace of Je - sus, Deep - er than the
the match-less grace of Je - sus,

Wonderful Grace of Jesus

the roll - ing sea;
might - y roll - ing sea;
Won - - - der - ful
High - er than the moun-tain,
grace,
spark - ling like a foun - tain,
all - suf - fi - cient for
All - suf - fi - cient grace for e - ven
me, for e - ven me,
me,
Broad - er than the scope of my trans -
trans -
gres - sions,
gres-sions, sing it!
Great - er far than all my sin and shame,
my sin and shame,
Oh, mag - ni - fy the pre - cious name of Je - sus, Praise His name!

Count Your Blessings

50

Many, . . . are thy wonderful works . . . more than can be numbered. Psa. 40:5

BLESSINGS 11.11.11.11. with Refrain

Johnson Oatman, Jr., 1856-1926

Edwin O. Excell, 1851-1921

1. When up-on life's bil-lows you are tem-pest-tossed, When you are dis-
2. Are you ev-er bur-dened with a load of care? Does the cross seem
3. When you look at oth-ers with their lands and gold, Think that Christ has
4. So, a-mid the con-flict, wheth-er great or small, Do not be dis-

cour-aged, think-ing all is lost, Count your man-y bless-ings, name them
heav-y you are called to bear? Count your man-y bless-ings, ev-ery
prom-ised you His wealth un-told; Count your man-y bless-ings, wealth can
heart-ened—God is o-ver all; Count your man-y bless-ings, an-gels

one by one, And it will sur-prise you what the Lord hath done.
doubt will fly, And you will keep sing-ing as the days go by.
nev-er buy Your re-ward in heav-en, nor your home on high.
will at-tend, Help and com-fort give you to your jour-ney's end.

REFRAIN

Count your bless-ings, name them one by one; Count your
Count your man-y bless-ings, name them one by one; Count your man-y

bless-ings, see what God hath done! Count your bless-ings,
bless-ings, see what God hath done! Count your man-y bless-ings,

name them one by one; Count your man-y bless-ings, see what God hath done.
see what God hath done.

Count Your Blessings

Fairest Lord Jesus

Thou art fairer than the children of men ... Psa. 45:2

CRUSADERS' HYMN P.M.
Silesian folk song
From *Schlesische Volkslieder*, 1842
Arranged by James Hopkirk, 19th century

Stanza 1, 3 from *Gesangbuch*, Münster, 1677
Stanza 2 trans. by Heinrich von Fallersleben, 1798-1874
Stanza 4 trans. by Joseph A. Seiss, 1823-1904

51

1. Fair - est Lord Je - sus, Rul - er of all na - ture, O Thou of
2. Fair are the mead-ows, Fair - er still the wood-lands, Robed in the
3. Fair is the sun-shine, Fair - er still the moon-light, And fair the
4. All fair - est beau - ty Heav-en - ly and earth-ly, Won-drous-ly,

God and man the Son; Thee will I cher - ish,
bloom - ing garb of spring; Je - sus is fair - er,
twink - ling, star - ry host; Je - sus shines bright - er,
Je - sus, is found in Thee; None can be near - er,

Thee will I hon - or, Thou my soul's glo - ry, joy, and crown.
Je - sus is pur - er, Who makes the woe - ful heart to sing.
Je - sus shines pur - er, Than all the an - gels heaven can boast.
fair - er or dear - er, Than Thou, my Sav - iour, art to me. A-MEN.

Jesus Is All the World to Me

. . . I count all things but loss for the excellency of the knowledge of Christ . . . Phil. 3:8

ELIZABETH Irregular
Will L. Thompson, 1847-1909
Will L. Thompson, 1847-1909

1. Je - sus is all the world to me, My life, my joy, my all;
2. Je - sus is all the world to me, My friend in tri - als sore;
3. Je - sus is all the world to me, And true to Him I'll be;
4. Je - sus is all the world to me, I want no bet - ter friend;

He is my strength from day to day, With - out Him I would fall.
I go to Him for bless - ings and He gives them o'er and o'er.
Oh, how could I this friend de - ny When He's so true to me?
I trust Him now, I'll trust Him when Life's fleet - ing days shall end.

When I am sad, to Him I go, No oth - er one can cheer me so;
He sends the sun-shine and the rain, He sends the har - vest's gold - en grain;
Fol - low - ing Him I know I'm right, He watch-es o'er me day and night;
Beau - ti - ful life with such a friend, Beau - ti - ful life that has no end;

When I am sad He makes me glad—He's my friend.
Sun - shine and rain, har - vest of grain—He's my friend.
Fol - low - ing Him by day and night—He's my friend.
E - ter - nal life, e - ter - nal joy! He's my friend!

What a Friend We Have in Jesus

. . . let your requests be made known unto God. Phil. 4:6

FRIENDSHIP 8.7.8.7.D.

Joseph M. Scriven, 1819-1886

Charles C. Converse, 1832-1918

1. What a friend we have in Je-sus, All our sins and griefs to bear!
2. Have we tri-als and temp-ta-tions? Is there trou-ble an-y-where?
3. Are we weak and heav-y-la-den, Cum-bered with a load of care?

What a priv-i-lege to car-ry Ev-ery-thing to God in prayer!
We should nev-er be dis-cour-aged—Take it to the Lord in prayer.
Pre-cious Sav-iour, still our ref-uge— Take it to the Lord in prayer.

Oh, what peace we oft-en for-feit, Oh, what need-less pain we bear,
Can we find a friend so faith-ful Who will all our sor-rows share?
Do thy friends de-spise, for-sake thee? Take it to the Lord in prayer;

All be-cause we do not car-ry Ev-ery-thing to God in prayer!
Je-sus knows our ev-ery weak-ness—Take it to the Lord in prayer.
In His arms He'll take and shield thee; Thou wilt find a sol-ace there.

Send Refreshing

That he might sanctify and cleanse it with the washing of water by the word. Eph. 5:26

Daniel W. Whittle, 1840-1901

Arthur B. Hunt, 1890-1971

1. Heaven-ly Fa - ther, we Thy chil - dren, Gath-ered round our ris - en Lord,
2. Gra - cious gales of heaven-ly bless - ing In Thy love to us af - ford;
3. Weak and wea - ry in the con - flict, Wres-tling "not with flesh and blood,"
4. With Thy strength, O Mas - ter, gird us; Be our guide and be our guard;

Lift our hearts in ear - nest plead - ing— Oh, re - vive us by Thy Word!
Let us feel Thy Spir - it's pres - ence— Oh, re - vive us by Thy Word!
Help us, Lord, as faint we fal - ter— Oh, re - vive us by Thy Word!
Fill us with Thy Ho - ly Spir - it— Oh, re - vive us by Thy Word!

REFRAIN

Send re - fresh - ing, send re - fresh - ing From Thy pres - ence, gra - cious Lord!

Send re - fresh - ing, send re - fresh - ing And re - vive us by Thy Word!

I Surrender All

. . . Lo, we have left all, and have followed thee. Mark 10:28

Judson W. Van De Venter, 1855-1939

SURRENDER 8.7.8.7. with Refrain
Winfield S. Weeden, 1847-1908

1. All to Je-sus I sur-ren-der; All to Him I free-ly give.
2. All to Je-sus I sur-ren-der; Hum-bly at His feet I bow,
3. All to Je-sus I sur-ren-der; Make me, Sav-iour, whol-ly Thine;
4. All to Je-sus I sur-ren-der; Lord, I give my-self to Thee.
5. All to Je-sus I sur-ren-der; Now I feel the sa-cred flame.
I will ev-er love and trust Him, In His pres-ence dai-ly live.
World-ly pleas-ures all for-sak-en. Take me, Je-sus, take me now.
Let me feel the Ho-ly Spir-it, Tru-ly know that Thou art mine.
Fill me with Thy love and pow-er; Let Thy bless-ing fall on me.
Oh, the joy of full sal-va-tion! Glo-ry, glo-ry to His name!
REFRAIN
I sur-ren-der all. I sur-ren-der all.
All to Thee, my bless-ed Sav-iour, I sur-ren-der all.

56 Have Thine Own Way, Lord!

. . . as the clay is in the potter's hand, so are ye in mine hand . . . Jer. 18:6

Adelaide A. Pollard, 1862-1934

ADELAIDE 5.4.5.4.D.
George C. Stebbins, 1846-1945

1. Have Thine own way, Lord! Have Thine own way! Thou art the
2. Have Thine own way, Lord! Have Thine own way! Search me and
3. Have Thine own way, Lord! Have Thine own way! Wound-ed and
4. Have Thine own way, Lord! Have Thine own way! Hold o'er my
Pot - ter, I am the clay. Mold me and make me
try me, Mas - ter, to - day! Whit - er than snow, Lord,
wea - ry, Help me I pray! Pow - er— all pow - er—
be - ing Ab - so - lute sway! Fill with Thy Spir - it
Aft - er Thy will, While I am wait - ing Yield-ed and still.
Wash me just now, As in Thy pres - ence Hum-bly I bow.
Sure - ly is Thine! Touch me and heal me, Sav - iour di - vine!
Till all shall see Christ on - ly, al - ways, Liv - ing in me!

Close to Thee

Close to Thee
He that saith, he abideth in him ought himself also so to walk . . . 1 John 2:6
Fanny J. Crosby, 1820-1915
Silas J. Vail, 1818-1884

1. Thou, my ev - er - last - ing por - tion, More than friend or life to me;
2. Not for ease or world - ly pleas - ure, Nor for fame my prayer shall be;
3. Lead me through the vale of shad-ows, Bear me o'er life's fit - ful sea;

All a - long my pil - grim jour - ney, Sav - iour, let me walk with Thee.
Glad - ly will I toil and suf - fer, On - ly let me walk with Thee.
Then the gate of life e - ter - nal May I en - ter, Lord, with Thee.

REFRAIN

Close to Thee, close to Thee, Close to Thee, close to Thee;
Close to Thee, close to Thee, Close to Thee, close to Thee;
Close to Thee, close to Thee, Close to Thee, close to Thee;

All a - long my pil - grim jour - ney, Sav - iour, let me walk with Thee.
Glad - ly will I toil and suf - fer, On - ly let me walk with Thee.
Then the gate of life e - ter - nal May I en - ter, Lord, with Thee.

Oh, to Be Like Thee, Blessed Redeemer

. . . to be conformed to the image of his Son . . . Rom 8:29

Thomas O. Chisholm, 1866-1960

CHRISTLIKE 10.9.10.9. with Refrain
William J. Kirkpatrick, 1838-1921

1. Oh, to be like Thee! bless-ed Re-deem-er, This is my con-stant
2. Oh, to be like Thee! full of com-pas-sion, Lov-ing, for-giv-ing,
3. Oh, to be like Thee! low-ly in spir-it, Ho-ly and harm-less,
4. Oh, to be like Thee! while I am plead-ing, Pour out Thy Spir-it,

long-ing and prayer. Glad-ly I'll for-feit all of earth's treas-ures,
ten-der, and kind, Help-ing the help-less, cheer-ing the faint-ing,
pa-tient and brave; Meek-ly en-dur-ing cru-el re-proach-es,
fill with Thy love; Make me a tem-ple meet for Thy dwell-ing,

Je-sus, Thy per-fect like-ness to wear.
Seek-ing the wan-dering sin-ner to find.
Will-ing to suf-fer oth-ers to save.
Fit me for life and heav-en a-bove.

REFRAIN

Oh, to be like Thee!

Oh, to be like Thee, Bless-ed Re-deem-er, pure as Thou art! Come in Thy
sweet-ness, come in Thy full-ness; Stamp Thine own im-age deep on my heart.

Deeper and Deeper

59

O the depth of the riches both of the wisdom and knowledge of God! .. Rom. 11:33

Oswald J. Smith, b. 1890

Oswald J. Smith, b. 1890

1. In - to the heart of Je - sus, deep - er and deep - er I go,
2. In - to the will of Je - sus, deep - er and deep - er I go,
3. In - to the cross of Je - sus, deep - er and deep - er I go,
4. In - to the joy of Je - sus, deep - er and deep - er I go,
5. In - to the love of Je - sus, deep - er and deep - er I go,
Seek - ing to know the rea - son why He should love me so—
Pray - ing for grace to fol - low, seek - ing His way to know;
Fol - low - ing through the gar - den, fac - ing the dread - ed foe—
Ris - ing with soul en - rap - tured far from the world be - low;
Prais - ing the One who brought me out of my sin and woe;
Why He should stoop to lift me up from the mir - y clay,
Bow - ing in full sur - ren - der low at His bless - ed feet,
Drink - ing the cup of sor - row, sob - bing with brok - en heart;
Joy in the place of sor - row, peace in the midst of pain,
And through e - ter - nal a - ges grate - ful - ly I shall sing;
Sav - ing my soul, mak - ing me whole, Though I had wan-dered a - way.
Bid - ding Him take, break me and make, Till I am mold-ed and meet.
"O Sav - iour, help! Dear Sav - iour, help! Grace for my weak-ness im - part."
Je - sus will give, Je - sus will give, He will up-hold and sus - tain.
"Oh, how He loved! Oh, how He loved! Je - sus, my Lord and my King."

Search Me, O God

. . . and know my heart: try me, and know my thoughts. Psa. 139:23

Albert B. Simpson, 1843-1919

Melody by Albert B. Simpson, 1843-1919

1. Search me, O God, search me and know my heart; Try me and prove me
2. Thou art the same to-day and yes-ter-day: Oh, make Thy life in
3. Take my poor heart and on-ly let me love The things that al-ways
4. Help me to lay my treas-ures up on high; Teach me to seek my
5. Oh, let my work a-bide the test-ing day That shall con-sume the

in the hid-den part; Cleanse me and make me ho-ly, as Thou
me the same al-way. Take from my heart the things that pass a-
shall a-bid-ing prove. Bind all my heart-strings to the world a-
fu-ture in the sky; Give me my por-tion yon-der by and
stub-ble and the hay; Oh, build my house up-on the Rock I

REFRAIN

art, And lead me in the way ev-er-last-ing.
way; Lead, lead me in the way ev-er-last-ing.
bove, And lead me in the way ev-er-last-ing. Lead me,
by— And lead me in the way ev-er-last-ing.
pray— And lead me in the way ev-er-last-ing.

lead me, lead me in the way ev-er-last-ing; Keep me from the

things that with-er and de-cay; Give to me the things that

can - not pass a - way—And lead me in the way ev - er - last - ing.

Thy Holy Spirit, Lord, Alone 61

. . . the Spirit is life because of righteousness. Rom. 8:10

Henrietta E. Blair, 19th century

William J. Kirkpatrick, 1838-1921

1. Thy Ho - ly Spir - it, Lord, a - lone Can turn our hearts from sin;
2. Thy Ho - ly Spir - it, Lord, a - lone Can deep - er love in - spire;
3. Thy Ho - ly Spir - it, Lord, can bring The gifts we seek in prayer;
4. Thy Ho - ly Spir - it, Lord, can give The grace we need this hour;

His power a - lone can sanc - ti - fy And keep us pure with - in.
His power a - lone with - in our souls Can light the sa - cred fire.
His voice can words of com - fort speak And still each wave of care.
And while we wait, O Spir - it, come In sanc - ti - fy - ing power.

REFRAIN
1-3. O Spir - it of faith and love, Come in our midst, we pray,
4. O Spir - it of love, de - scend; Come in our midst, we pray,

And pu - ri - fy each wait - ing heart; Bap - tize us with power to - day.
And like a rush - ing, might - y wind Sweep o - ver our souls to - day.

Draw Me Nearer

But it is good for me to draw near to God ... Psa. 73:28

I AM THINE 10.7.10.7. with Refrain
William H. Doane, 1832-1915

Fanny J. Crosby, 1820-1915

1. I am Thine, O Lord, I have heard Thy voice, And it
2. Con - se - crate me now to Thy serv - ice, Lord, By the
3. Oh, the pure de - light of a sin - gle hour That be -
4. There are depths of love that I can - not know Till I
told Thy love to me; But I long to rise in the arms of faith
power of grace di - vine; Let my soul look up with a stead-fast hope,
fore Thy throne I spend, When I kneel in prayer, and with Thee, my God,
cross the nar - row sea; There are heights of joy that I may not reach
And be clos - er drawn to Thee.
And my will be lost in Thine.
I com - mune as friend with friend!
Till I rest in peace with Thee.
REFRAIN
Draw me near - er,
near - er, bless - ed Lord, To the cross where Thou hast died; Draw me
near - er, near - er, near - er, bless - ed Lord, To Thy pre - cious, bleed - ing side.

Himself

. . . Christ is all, and in all. Col. 3:11

Albert B. Simpson, 1843-1919

Albert B. Simpson, 1843-1919

1. Once it was the bless-ing, Now it is the Lord; Once it was the feel-ing,
2. Once 'twas pain-ful try-ing, Now 'tis per-fect trust; Once a half sal-va-tion,
3. Once 'twas bus-y plan-ning, Now 'tis trust-ful prayer; Once 'twas anxious car-ing,
4. Once it was my work-ing, His it hence shall be; Once I tried to use Him,
5. Once I hoped in Je-sus, Now I know He's mine; Once my lamps were dy-ing,

Now it is His Word; Once His gift I want-ed, Now the Giv-er own;
Now the ut-ter-most! Once 'twas cease-less hold-ing, Now He holds me fast;
Now He has the care; Once 'twas what I want-ed, Now what Je-sus says;
Now He us-es me; Once the power I want-ed, Now the Might-y One;
Now they bright-ly shine; Once for death I wait-ed, Now His com-ing hail;

Once I sought for heal-ing, Now Him-self a-lone.
Once 'twas con-stant drift-ing, Now my an-chor's cast.
Once 'twas con-stant ask-ing, Now 'tis cease-less praise. All in all for-ev-er,
Once for self I la-bored, Now for Him a-lone.
And my hopes are an-chored Safe with-in the vail.

Je-sus will I sing; Ev-ery-thing in Je-sus, And Je-sus ev-ery-thing.

Breathe upon Us

. . . he breathed on them, . . . Receive ye the Holy Ghost. John 20:22

Russell K. Carter, 1849-1928

Melody by Russell K. Carter, 1849-1928
Harmony by J. Buchanan MacMillan, b. 1915

1. Breathe up - on us, Lord, from heav - en, Fill us with the Ho - ly Ghost;
2. While the Spir - it hov - ers near us, O - pen all our hearts we pray;
3. Lift us, Lord, oh, lift us high - er, From the car - nal mind set free;

Prom - ise of the Fa - ther giv - en, Send us now a Pen - te - cost.
To Thine im - age, Lord, re - store us; Wit - ness in our souls to - day.
Fill us with re - fin - ing fire; Give us per - fect lib - er - ty.

REFRAIN

Breathe up - on us, breathe up - on us; With Thy love our hearts in - spire.

Breathe up - on us, breathe up - on us; Lord, bap - tize us now with fire.

Harmony copyright 1961 by Christian Publications, Inc.

Fill Me Now

65

... be filled with the Spirit. Eph. 5:18

Elwood H. Stokes, 1815-1895

FILL ME NOW 8.7.8.7. with Refrain
John R. Sweney, 1837-1899

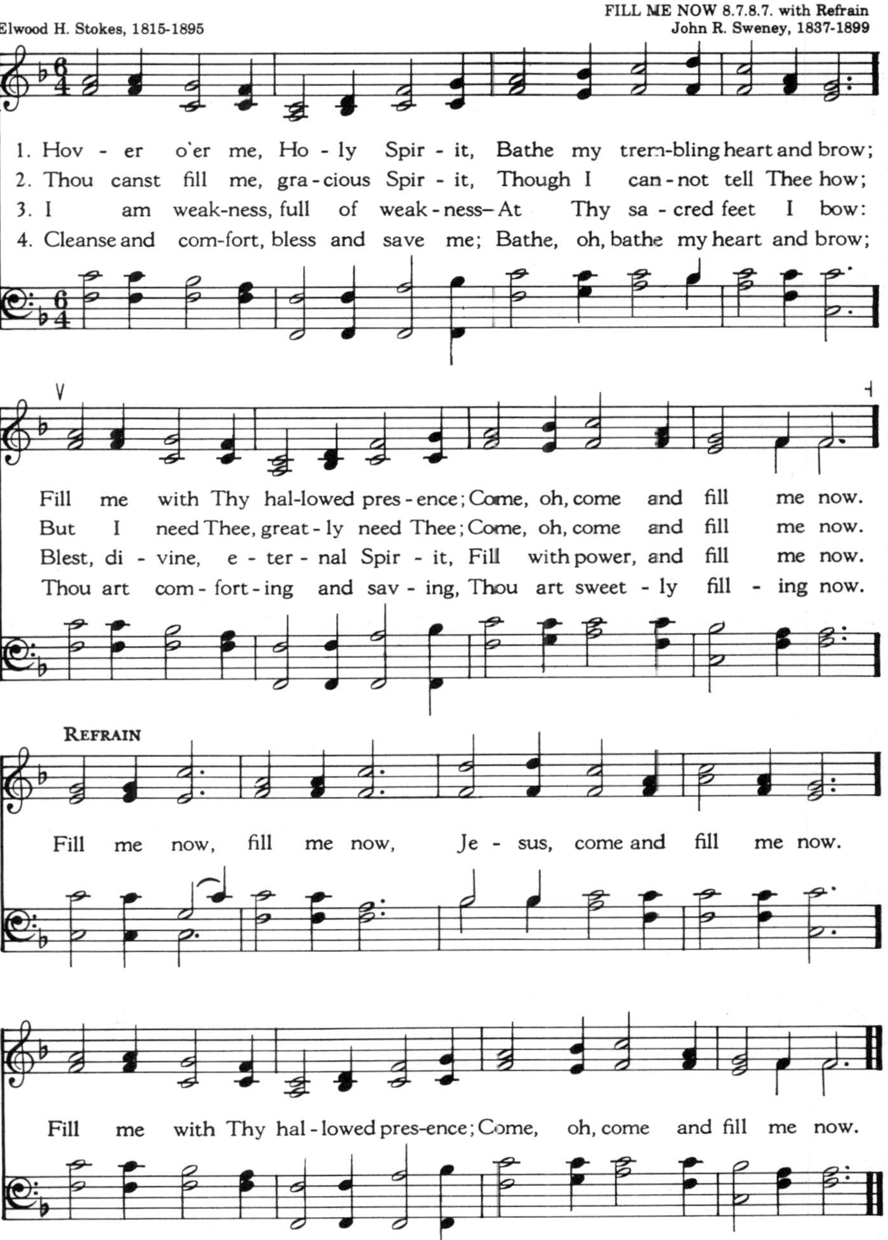

1. Hov - er o'er me, Ho - ly Spir - it, Bathe my trem-bling heart and brow;
2. Thou canst fill me, gra - cious Spir - it, Though I can - not tell Thee how;
3. I am weak-ness, full of weak - ness— At Thy sa - cred feet I bow:
4. Cleanse and com-fort, bless and save me; Bathe, oh, bathe my heart and brow;

Fill me with Thy hal-lowed pres - ence; Come, oh, come and fill me now.
But I need Thee, great - ly need Thee; Come, oh, come and fill me now.
Blest, di - vine, e - ter - nal Spir - it, Fill with power, and fill me now.
Thou art com - fort-ing and sav - ing, Thou art sweet - ly fill - ing now.

REFRAIN
Fill me now, fill me now, Je - sus, come and fill me now.

Fill me with Thy hal - lowed pres-ence; Come, oh, come and fill me now.

Jesus, I Am Resting, Resting

. . . ye shall find rest for your souls. . . . Jer. 6:16

Jean S. Pigott, 1845-1882

TRANQUILITY 8.7.8.5.D. with Refrain
James Mountain, 1843-1933

1. Je - sus, I am rest - ing, rest - ing In the joy of what Thou art;
2. Oh, how great Thy lov - ing kind - ness, Vast - er, broad-er than the sea!
3. Sim - ply trust - ing Thee, Lord Je - sus, I be - hold Thee as Thou art,
4. Ev - er lift Thy face up - on me, As I work and wait for Thee;

I am find - ing out the great - ness Of Thy lov - ing heart.
Oh, how mar - vel - ous Thy good - ness Lav - ished all on me!
And Thy love, so pure, so change - less, Sat - is - fies my heart;
Rest - ing 'neath Thy smile, Lord Je - sus, Earth's dark shad - ows flee.

Thou hast bid me gaze up - on Thee, And Thy beau - ty fills my soul;
Yes, I rest in Thee, Be - lov - ed, Know what wealth of grace is Thine,
Sat - is - fies its deep - est long - ings, Meets, sup-plies its ev - ery need,
Bright-ness of my Fa-ther's glo - ry, Sun - shine of my Fa - ther's face,

For, by Thy trans - form - ing pow - er, Thou hast made me whole.
Know Thy cer - tain - ty of prom - ise, And have made it mine.
Com - pass - eth me round with bless - ings: Thine is love in - deed!
Keep me ev - er trust - ing, rest - ing; Fill me with Thy grace.

Jesus, I Am Resting, Resting

Je - sus, I am rest - ing, rest - ing In the joy of what Thou art;
I am find - ing out the great - ness Of Thy lov - ing heart.

Thy Kingdom Come 67

. . . Thy will be done in earth, as it is in heaven. Matt. 6:10

PAROUSIA 6.6.6.4. with repeat

Albert B. Simpson, 1843-1919

Melody by Albert B. Simpson, 1843-1919

1. O Christ, my Lord and King, This is the prayer I bring,
2. Help me to work and pray, Help me to live each day
3. Up - on my heart's high throne, Rule Thou, and Thou a - lone;
4. Through all the earth a - broad, Wher - ev - er man has trod,
5. Soon may our King ap - pear! Haste bright mil - len - nial year!

This is the song I sing: Thy king-dom come, Thy king-dom come.
That all I do may say, Thy king-dom come, Thy king-dom come.
Let me be all Thine own! Thy king-dom come, Thy king-dom come.
Send forth Thy Word, O God— Thy king-dom come, Thy king-dom come.
We live to bring it near. Thy king-dom come, Thy king-dom come. A-MEN.

Wherever He Leads I'll Go

...I am the Lord thy God which ... leadeth thee ... Isa. 48:17

Baylus B. McKinney, 1886-1952

FALLS CREEK 8.6.8.7. with Refrain
Baylus B. McKinney, 1886-1952

1. "Take up thy cross and fol-low Me," I heard my Mas-ter say.
2. He drew me clos-er to His side. I sought His will to know,
3. It may be through the shad-ows dim, Or o'er the storm-y sea.
4. My heart, my life, my all I bring To Christ, who loves me so.

"I gave My life to ran-som thee; Sur-ren-der your all to-day."
And in that will I now a-bide; Wher-ev-er He leads I'll go.
I take my cross and fol-low Him, Wher-ev-er He lead-eth me.
He is my Mas-ter, Lord, and King; Wher-ev-er He leads I'll go.

REFRAIN
Wher-ev-er He leads I'll go; Wher-ev-er He leads I'll go.

I'll fol-low my Christ, who loves me so. Wher-ev-er He leads I'll go.

Where He Leads Me

69

... leaving us an example, that ye should follow his steps. 1 Pet. 2:21

NORRIS 8.8.8.9. with Refrain
John S. Norris, 1844-1907

E.W. Blandy, 19th century

1. I can hear my Sav-iour call-ing, I can hear my Sav-iour call-ing,
2. I'll go with Him through the gar-den, I'll go with Him through the gar-den,
3. I'll go with Him through the judg-ment, I'll go with Him through the judg-ment,
4. He will give me grace and glo-ry, He will give me grace and glo-ry,
REFRAIN
Where He leads me I will fol-low, Where He leads me I will fol-low,
D.C. for Refrain
I can hear my Sav-iour call-ing, "Take thy cross and fol-low, fol-low Me."
I'll go with Him through the gar-den; I'll go with Him, with Him all the way.
I'll go with Him through the judg-ment; I'll go with Him, with Him all the way.
He will give me grace and glo-ry And go with me, with me all the way.
Where He leads me I will fol-low, I'll go with Him, with Him all the way.

Alas, and Did My Saviour Bleed

70

... he was wounded for our transgressions ... Isa. 53:5

MARTYRDOM C.M.
Hugh Wilson, 1764-1824

Isaac Watts, 1674-1748

1. A-las, and did my Sav-iour bleed? And did my Sov-ereign die?
2. Was it for sins that I had done He groaned up-on the tree?
3. Well might the sun in dark-ness hide, And shut His glo-ries in,
4. But drops of grief can ne'er re-pay The debt of love I owe:
Would He de-vote that sa-cred head For such a worm as I?
A-maz-ing pit-y! Grace un-known! And love be-yond de-gree!
When Christ, the might-y Mak-er, died For man, the crea-ture's sin.
Here, Lord, I give my-self to Thee; 'Tis all that I can do. A-MEN.

Wilt Thou Be Made Whole?

. . . thy faith hath made thee whole . . . Mark 5:34

William J. Kirkpatrick, 1838-1921

William J. Kirkpatrick, 1838-1921

1. Hear the foot-steps of Je-sus— He is now pass-ing by,
2. 'Tis the voice of that Sav-iour, Whose mer-ci-ful call
3. Are you halt-ing and strug-gling, O-ver-powered by your sin,
4. Bless-ed Sav-iour, as-sist us To rest on Thy Word;

Bear-ing balm for the wound-ed, Heal-ing all who ap-ply;
Free-ly of-fers sal-va-tion To one and to all;
While the wa-ters are trou-bled Can you not en-ter in?
Let the soul-heal-ing pow-er On us now be out-poured;

As He spake to the suf-ferer Who lay at the pool,
He is now beck-oning to Him Each sin-taint-ed soul
Lo, the Sav-iour stands wait-ing To strength-en your soul;
Wash a-way ev-ery sin spot, Take per-fect con-trol,

He is say-ing this mo-ment, "Wilt thou be made whole?"
And lov-ing-ly ask-ing, "Wilt thou be made whole?"
He is ear-nest-ly plead-ing, "Wilt thou be made whole?"
Say to each trust-ing spir-it, "Thy faith makes thee whole."

Wilt Thou Be Made Whole?

REFRAIN
Wilt thou be made whole? Wilt thou be made whole?
Oh, come, wea - ry suf - ferer, Oh, come, sin - sick soul;
See the life - stream is flow - ing, See the cleans - ing waves roll;
Step in - to the cur - rent and thou shalt be whole.

Living in the Glory

...an entrance shall be ministered unto you ... into the everlasting kingdom ... 2 Pet. 1:11

Albert B. Simpson, 1843-1919

May A. Stephens, 1865-1935

1. I have found a heaven be - low, I am liv - ing in the glo - ry;
2. Storms of sor - row 'round me fall, But I'm liv - ing in the glo - ry;
3. Sa - tan can - not touch my heart While I'm liv - ing in the glo - ry;
4. I can tri - umph o - ver pain While I'm liv - ing in the glo - ry;
5. I am poor and lit - tle known, But I'm liv - ing in the glo - ry;
6. Soon the King will come for me To be with Him in the glo - ry;

Oh, the joy and strength I know, Liv - ing in the glo - ry of the Lord.
I can sing a - bove them all, Liv - ing in the glo - ry of the Lord.
This dis - arms each fier - y dart, Liv - ing in the glo - ry of the Lord.
I can count each loss a gain, Liv - ing in the glo - ry of the Lord.
And I'm wait - ing for a throne, Liv - ing in the glo - ry of the Lord.
Then my song shall sweet - er be, Reign - ing in the glo - ry of the Lord.

REFRAIN

Yes, I'm liv - ing in the glo - ry As He prom - ised in His Word;

I am dwell - ing in the heaven - lies, Liv - ing in the glo - ry of the Lord.

Near to the Heart of God

Draw nigh to God, and he will draw nigh to you. . . . James 4:8

Cleland B. McAfee, 1866-1944

MCAFEE C.M. with Refrain
Cleland B. McAfee, 1866-1944

1. There is a place of qui-et rest Near to the heart of God,
2. There is a place of com-fort sweet Near to the heart of God,
3. There is a place of full re-lease Near to the heart of God,
A place where sin can-not mo-lest, Near to the heart of God.
A place where we our Sav-iour meet, Near to the heart of God.
A place where all is joy and peace, Near to the heart of God.
REFRAIN
O Je-sus, blest Re-deem-er Sent from the heart of God,
Hold us, who wait be-fore Thee, Near to the heart of God.

At the Cross I'll Abide

Wash me throughly from mine iniquity, and cleanse me from my sin. Psa. 51:2

Isaiah Baltzell, 1832-1893

Isaiah Baltzell, 1832-1893

1. O Je - sus, Sav - iour, I long to rest Near the cross where Thou hast died;
2. My dy - ing Je - sus, my Sav - iour, God, Who hast borne my guilt and sin,
3. O Je - sus, Sav - iour, now make me Thine, Nev - er let me stray from Thee;
4. The cleans-ing power of Thy blood ap - ply, All my guilt and sin re - move;

For there is hope for the ach - ing breast; At the cross I will a - bide.
Now wash me, cleanse me with Thine own blood; Ev - er keep me pure and clean.
Oh, wash me, cleanse me, for Thou art mine, And Thy love is full and free.
Oh, help me, while at Thy cross I lie, Fill my soul with per - fect love.

REFRAIN
At the cross I'll a - bide, At the cross I'll a - bide; At the cross I'll a - bide, There His blood is ap - plied; At the cross I am sat - is - fied.

Blessed Assurance

. . . he hath given assurance unto all men . . . Acts 17:31

Fanny J. Crosby, 1820-1915

ASSURANCE 9.10.9.9. with Refrain
Phoebe P. Knapp, 1839-1908

1. Bless-ed as - sur - ance, Je - sus is mine! Oh, what a fore-taste of
2. Per - fect sub - mis - sion, per-fect de - light, Vi - sions of rap-ture now
3. Per - fect sub - mis - sion, all is at rest; I in my Sav - iour am

glo - ry di - vine! Heir of sal - va - tion, pur-chase of God, Born of His
burst on my sight. An - gels de - scend-ing, bring from a - bove Ech - oes of
hap - py and blest, Watch-ing and wait - ing, look-ing a - bove, Filled with His

Refrain

Spir - it, washed in His blood.
mer - cy, whis-pers of love. This is my sto - ry, this is my
good-ness, lost in His love.

song: Prais - ing my Sav - iour all the day long. This is my

sto - ry, this is my song: Prais-ing my Sav - iour all the day long.

It Is Well with My Soul

And the peace of God, . . . shall keep your hearts and minds through Christ Jesus. Phil. 4:7

Horatio G. Spafford, 1828-1888

VILLE DU HAVRE 11.8.11.9. with Refrain
Philip P. Bliss, 1838-1876

1. When peace like a riv - er at - tend - eth my way, When
2. Though Sa - tan should buf - fet, though tri - als should come, Let
3. My sin— oh, the bliss of this glo - ri - ous thought–My
4. And, Lord, haste the day when the faith shall be sight, The

sor - rows like sea bil - lows roll, What - ev - er my lot, Thou hast
this blest as - sur - ance con - trol, That Christ hath re - gard - ed my
sin, not in part but the whole, Is nailed to His cross and I
clouds be rolled back as a scroll, The trump shall re - sound, and the

taught me to say, "It is well, it is well with my soul."
help - less es - tate, And hath shed His own blood for my soul.
bear it no more! Praise the Lord, praise the Lord, O my soul!
Lord shall de - scend! E - ven so— it is well with my soul!

REFRAIN
It is well   with my soul;   it is well, it is well with my soul!
It is well   with my soul;

Like a River Glorious

...I will extend peace to her like a river ... Isa. 66:12

WYE VALLEY 6.5.6.5.D. with Refrain
Frances R. Havergal, 1836-1879
James Mountain, 1843-1933

1. Like a riv - er glo - rious Is God's per - fect peace, O - ver
2. Hid - den in the hol - low Of His bless - ed hand, Nev - er
3. Ev - ery joy or tri - al Fall - eth from a - bove, Traced up -

all vic - to - rious In its bright in - crease; Per - fect, yet it
foe can fol - low, Nev - er trai - tor stand. Not a surge of
on our di - al By the Sun of love. We may trust Him

flow - eth Full - er ev - ery day; Per - fect, yet it grow - eth
wor - ry, Not a shade of care, Not a blast of hur - ry
ful - ly— All for us to do; They who trust Him whol - ly

REFRAIN

Deep - er all the way.
Touch the spir - it there. Stayed up - on Je - ho - vah Hearts are
Find Him whol - ly true.

ful - ly blest, Find - ing, as He prom - ised, Per - fect peace and rest.

My Hope Is Built on Nothing Less

He ... set my feet upon a rock, and established my goings. Psa. 40:2

Edward Mote, 1797-1874

SOLID ROCK L.M. with Refrain
William B. Bradbury, 1816-1868

1. My hope is built on noth - ing less Than Je - sus' blood and
2. When dark-ness veils His love - ly face, I rest on His un -
3. His oath, His cov - e - nant, His blood Sup - port me in the
4. When He shall come with trum - pet sound, Oh, may I then in
right - eous - ness; I dare not trust the sweet - est frame But
chang - ing grace; In ev - ery high and storm - y gale My
whelm - ing flood; When all a - round my soul gives way, He
Him be found, Dressed in His right - eous - ness a - lone, Fault -
whol - ly lean on Je - sus' name.
an - chor holds with - in the veil.
then is all my hope and stay.
less to stand be - fore the throne!
REFRAIN
On Christ, the sol - id rock I stand;
All oth - er ground is sink-ing sand, All oth - er ground is sink - ing sand.

I Know Whom I Have Believed

. . . and am persuaded that he is able . . . 2 Tim. 1:12

Daniel W. Whittle, 1840-1901

EL NATHAN C.M. with Refrain
James McGranahan, 1840-1907

1. I know not why God's won-drous grace To me He hath made known,
2. I know not how this sav-ing faith To me He did im-part,
3. I know not how the Spir-it moves, Con-vinc-ing men of sin,
4. I know not what of good or ill May be re-served for me,
5. I know not when my Lord may come, At night or noon-day fair,

Nor why—un-wor-thy—Christ in love Re-deemed me for His own.
Nor how be-liev-ing in His Word Wrought peace with-in my heart.
Re-veal-ing Je-sus through the Word, Cre-a-ting faith in Him.
Of wea-ry ways or gold-en days, Be-fore His face I see.
Nor if I walk the vale with Him Or meet Him in the air.

REFRAIN

But "I know whom I have be-liev-ed, And am per-suad-ed that He is

a-ble To keep that which I've com-mit-ted Un-to Him a-gainst that day."

80

My Anchor Holds

. . . we have . . . an anchor of the soul, both sure and stedfast . . . Heb. 6:19

MY ANCHOR HOLDS 7.7.7.7. with Refrain

W.C. Martin, 19th century

Daniel B. Towner, 1850-1919

1. Though the an-gry sur-ges roll On my tem-pest-driv-en soul,
2. Might-y tides a-bout me sweep, Per-ils lurk with-in the deep,
3. I can feel the an-chor fast As I meet each sud-den blast,
4. Trou-bles al-most 'whelm the soul; Griefs like bil-lows o'er me roll;

I am peace-ful, for I know, Wild-ly though the winds may blow,
An-gry clouds o'er-shade the sky, And the tem-pest ris-es high;
And the ca-ble, though un-seen, Bears the heav-y strain be-tween;
Tempt-ers seek to lure a-stray; Storms ob-scure the light of day—

I've an an-chor safe and sure That can ev-er-more en-dure.
Still I stand the tem-pest's shock, For my an-chor grips the rock.
Through the storm I safe-ly ride Till the turn-ing of the tide.
But in Christ I can be bold; I've an an-chor that shall hold.

REFRAIN
And it holds, my an-chor holds; Blow your wild-est, then, O
And it holds, my an-chor holds; Blow your wild - - est,

My Anchor Holds

gale, On my bark so small and frail; By His grace I shall not
gale, O gale,
fail, For my an - chor holds, my an - chor holds.
For my an - chor holds, it firm - ly holds,

Hallelujah, What a Saviour! 81

He is despised and rejected of men; a man of sorrows . . . Isa. 53:3

MAN OF SORROWS 7.7.7.8.
Philip P. Bliss, 1838-1876

Philip P. Bliss, 1838-1876

1. "Man of sor-rows," what a name For the Son of God who came,
2. Bear - ing shame and scof-fing rude, In my place con-demned He stood,
3. Guilt - y, vile, and help-less we; Spot-less Lamb of God was He;
4. Lift - ed up was He to die; "It is fin-ished," was His cry,
5. When He comes, our glo-rious King, All His ran-somed home to bring,

Ru - ined sin-ners to re - claim! Hal - le - lu - jah! What a Sav - iour!
Sealed my par - don with His blood; Hal - le - lu - jah! What a Sav - iour!
"Full a - tone-ment," can it be! Hal - le - lu - jah! What a Sav - iour!
Now in heaven ex - alt - ed high; Hal - le - lu - jah! What a Sav - iour!
Then a - new this song we'll sing, Hal - le - lu - jah! What a Sav - iour!

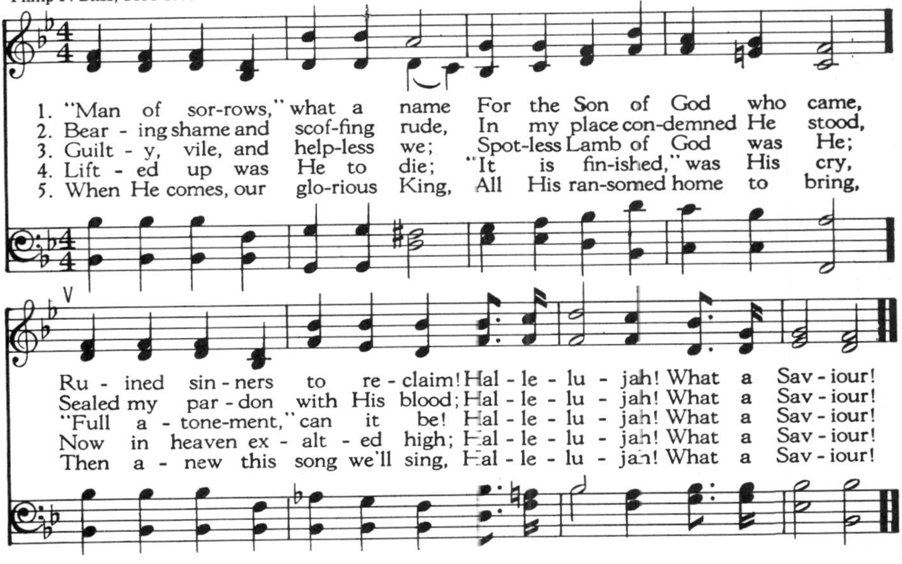

Nothing Is Too Hard for Jesus

Ah Lord God! . . . there is nothing too hard for thee. Jer. 32:17

Albert B. Simpson, 1843-1919

Albert B. Simpson, 1843-1919

1. Oft there comes a won-drous mes-sage When my hopes are grow-ing dim,
2. When my frame is worn with sick-ness And with tears my eye-lids swim,
3. When my way is closed in dark-ness And my foes are fierce and grim,
4. When my heart is crushed with an-guish And the wa-ters reach the brim,
5. Let us claim the might-y prom-ise, Let us light the torch-es dim.
I can hear it through the dark-ness Like some sweet and far-off hymn.
I can hear the prom-ise ring-ing Like some sweet and heaven-ly hymn.
Still it sings a-bove the con-flict Like some glad, vic-to-rious hymn.
Faith can hear the might-y cho-rus Like some might-y bat-tle hymn.
Let us join the might-y cho-rus, Let us swell the glo-rious hymn.
REFRAIN
Noth-ing is too hard for Je-sus, No man can work like Him;
Noth-ing is too hard for Je-sus, No man can work like Him.

Just As I Am, without One Plea

83

WOODWORTH 8.8.8.6.2.
William B. Bradbury, 1816-1868
Charlotte Elliott, 1789-1871
... come ... without money and without price. Isa. 55:1

1. Just as I am, with-out one plea, But that Thy blood was shed for me, And that Thou bidd'st me come to Thee, O Lamb of God, I come, I come!
2. Just as I am and wait-ing not To rid my soul of one dark blot, To Thee, whose blood can cleanse each spot, O Lamb of God, I come, I come!
3. Just as I am, though tossed a-bout With man-y a con-flict, man-y a doubt, Fight-ings with-in, and fears with-out, O Lamb of God, I come, I come!
4. Just as I am, Thou wilt re-ceive, Wilt wel-come, par-don, cleanse, re-lieve; Be-cause Thy prom-ise I be-lieve, O Lamb of God, I come, I come!
5. Just as I am, Thy love un-known Hath bro-ken ev-ery bar-rier down; Now, to be Thine, yea, Thine a-lone, O Lamb of God, I come, I come!

84
Faith Is the Victory
. . . this is the victory that overcometh the world, even our faith. 1 John 5:4
John H. Yates, 1837-1900
SANKEY C.M.D. with Refrain
Ira D. Sankey, 1840-1908
1. En - camped a - long the hills of light, Ye Chris - tian sol - diers, rise,
2. His ban - ner o - ver us is love, Our sword the Word of God;
3. On ev - ery hand the foe we find Drawn up in dread ar - ray;
4. To him that o - ver - comes the foe White rai - ment shall be given;
And press the bat - tle ere the night Shall veil the glow - ing skies.
We tread the road the saints a - bove With shouts of tri - umph trod.
Let tents of ease be left be - hind, And on - ward to the fray;
Be - fore the an - gels he shall know His name con - fessed in heaven.
A - gainst the foe in vales be - low, Let all our strength be hurled;
By faith they, like a whirl-wind's breath, Swept on o'er ev - ery field;
Sal - va - tion's hel - met on each head, With truth all girt a - bout,
Then on - ward from the hills of light, Our hearts with love a - flame,
Faith is the vic - to - ry, we know, That o - ver - comes the world.
The faith by which they con - quered death Is still our shin - ing shield.
The earth shall trem - ble 'neath our tread And ech - o with our shout.
We'll van - quish all the hosts of night In Je - sus' con - quering name.
REFRAIN
Faith is the vic - to - ry! Faith is the vic - to - ry!

Faith Is the Victory

Oh, glo-ri-ous vic-to-ry That o-ver-comes the world.

Revive Us Again

. . . that thy people may rejoice . . . Psa. 85:6

85

REVIVE US AGAIN 11.11. with Refrain

William P. Mackay, 1839-1885

John J. Husband, 1760-1825

1. We praise Thee, O God, for the Son of Thy love, For Je-sus who
2. We praise Thee, O God, for Thy Spir-it of light, Who has shown us our
3. All glo-ry and praise to the Lamb that was slain, Who has borne all our
4. Re-vive us a-gain, fill each heart with Thy love; May each soul be re-
REFRAIN
died and is now gone a-bove.
Sav-iour and scat-tered our night. Hal-le-lu-jah! Thine the glo-ry, Hal-le-
sins and has cleansed ev-ery stain.
kin-dled with fire from a-bove.
lu-jah! A-men; Hal-le-lu-jah! Thine the glo-ry; Re-vive us a-gain.

Jesus Giveth Us the Victory

...thanks be to God ... 1 Cor. 15:57

Albert B. Simpson, 1843-1919

Melody by Albert B. Simpson, 1843-1919

1. There's a bat - tle rag - ing in the heaven-ly plac - es, Sin and
2. Faith can hear our Cap - tain call - ing from the heav - ens, "Cour-age,
3. We are led by One who nev - er lost a bat - tle, And our
4. Let us take the vic - tory o - ver Sa - tan's king-dom, O - ver

death and sick - ness with Sa - tan lead - ing on; With the hosts of
broth-er, I have o - ver-come for you; Fear not, I am
ad - ver - sar - y is a con-quered foe; We are more than
sick - ness, sor - row, self, and sin; Let us bear the

earth and hell ar-rayed a - gainst us, How in all our weak-ness
with you, I will nev - er fail you; Trust-ing in My prom - ise,
con-querors through our Cap-tain's tri - umph; Let us shout the vic - tory
ban - ner o'er the lands of dark - ness, Till the foes' last strong-hold

REFRAIN

shall the fight be won?
you shall con - quer too." Je - sus giv - eth us the vic - to - ry.
as we on - ward go.
we for Christ shall win.

He, who o - ver-came on Cal - va - ry, O-ver-comes a - gain in

Jesus Giveth Us the Victory

you and me. Hal - le - lu - jah! Je - sus gives the vic - to - ry!

The Branch of Healing   87

. . . for I am the Lord that healeth thee. Exod. 15:26

RETREAT L.M.

Albert B. Simpson, 1843-1919

Melody by Thomas Hastings, 1784-1872

1. There is a heal - ing branch that grows Where ev - ery
2. There is an old ap - point - ed way For those who
3. There is an ord' - nance that has stood Since Is - rael
4. There is a great Phy - si - cian still Whose hand has

bit - ter Ma - rah flows; This is our health - re-
heark - en and o - bey; A - bove the gate these
crossed the part - ed flood; It stands to - day for
all its an - cient skill; At His com - mand our

new - ing tree. "I am the Lord that heal - eth thee."
words we see: "I am the Lord that heal - eth thee."
you and me— "I am the Lord that heal - eth thee."
pains will flee— "I am the Lord that heal - eth thee."

Guide Me, O Thou Great Jehovah

... he will be our guide even unto death. Psa. 48:14

From the Welsh of William Williams, 1717-1791
Stanza 1 Trans. by Peter Williams, 1722-1796
Stanzas 2-3 Trans. by William Williams, 1717-1791

CWM RHONDDA 8.7.8.7.8.7. with repeat
John Hughes, 1873-1932

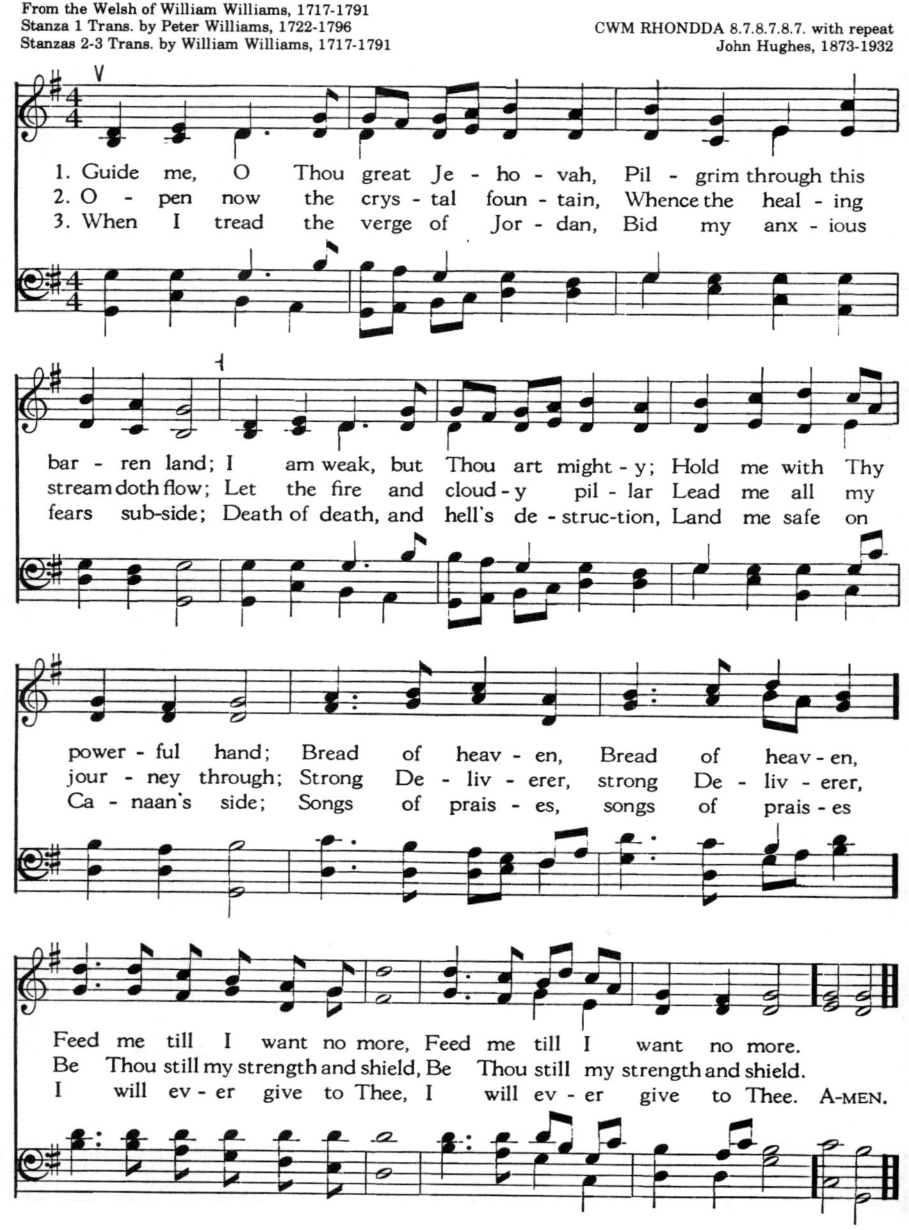

1. Guide me, O Thou great Je - ho - vah, Pil - grim through this
2. O - pen now the crys - tal foun - tain, Whence the heal - ing
3. When I tread the verge of Jor - dan, Bid my anx - ious

bar - ren land; I am weak, but Thou art might - y; Hold me with Thy
stream doth flow; Let the fire and cloud - y pil - lar Lead me all my
fears sub-side; Death of death, and hell's de - struc-tion, Land me safe on

power - ful hand; Bread of heav - en, Bread of heav - en,
jour - ney through; Strong De - liv - erer, strong De - liv - erer,
Ca - naan's side; Songs of prais - es, songs of prais - es

Feed me till I want no more, Feed me till I want no more.
Be Thou still my strength and shield, Be Thou still my strength and shield.
I will ev - er give to Thee, I will ev - er give to Thee. A-MEN.

Onward, Christian Soldiers

... endure hardness, as a good soldier of Jesus Christ. 2 Tim. 2:3

Sabine Baring-Gould, 1834-1924

ST. GERTRUDE 6.5.6.5.D. with Refrain
Arthur S. Sullivan, 1842-1900

1. On - ward, Chris - tian sol - diers, March-ing as to war, With the cross of Je - sus
2. Like a might-y ar - my Moves the Church of God; Broth-ers, we are tread - ing
3. Crowns and thrones may per-ish, King-doms rise and wane, But the Church of Je - sus
4. On - ward, then, ye peo-ple, Join our hap-py throng, Blend with ours your voic-es
Go - ing on be - fore: Christ, the roy - al Mas - ter, Leads a - gainst the foe;
Where the saints have trod; We are not di - vid - ed, All one bod - y we,
Con - stant will re-main; Gates of hell can nev - er 'Gainst that Church pre-vail;
In the tri-umph song; Glo - ry, laud, and hon - or Un - to Christ the King;
REFRAIN
For - ward in - to bat - tle, See His ban-ners go.
One in hope and doc - trine, One in char - i - ty. On-ward, Chris-tian sol - diers,
We have Christ's own prom-ise, And that can - not fail.
This through countless a - ges Men and an - gels sing.
March-ing as to war, With the cross of Je - sus Go - ing on be - fore.

Channels Only

... he shall be a vessel ... meet for the master's use ... 2 Tim. 2:21

CHANNELS 8.7.8.7. with Refrain

Mary E. Maxwell, 20th century

Ada R. Gibbs, 1865-1905

1. How I praise Thee, pre-cious Sav-iour, That Thy love laid hold of me;
2. Emp-tied that Thou should-est fill me, A clean ves-sel in Thy hand;
3. Wit-ness-ing Thy power to save me, Set-ting free from self and sin,
4. Je-sus, fill now with Thy Spir-it Hearts that full sur-ren-der know;

Thou hast saved and cleansed and filled me That I might Thy chan-nel be.
With no power but as Thou giv-est Gra-cious-ly with each com-mand.
Thou who bought-est to pos-sess me, In Thy full-ness, Lord, come in.
That the streams of liv-ing wa-ter From our in-ner man may flow.

REFRAIN

Chan-nels on-ly, bless-ed Mas-ter, But with all Thy won-drous power

Flow-ing through us, Thou canst use us Ev-ery day and ev-ery hour.

The Church's One Foundation

For other foundation can no man lay than that is laid, which is Jesus Christ. 1 Cor. 3:11

Samuel J. Stone, 1839-1900

AURELIA 7.6.7.6.D.
Samuel S. Wesley, 1810-1876

1. The Church's one Foun - da - tion Is Je - sus Christ her Lord;
2. E - lect from ev - ery na - tion Yet one o'er all the earth,
3. Though with a scorn - ful won - der Men see her sore op - pressed,
4. 'Mid toil and trib - u - la - tion And tu - mult of her war,
5. Yet she on earth hath un - ion With God the Three - in - One,

She is His new cre - a - tion By wa - ter and the Word:
Her char - ter of sal - va - tion, One Lord, one faith, one birth;
By schis - ms rent a - sun - der, By her - e - sies dis - tressed,
She waits the con - sum - ma - tion Of peace for - ev - er - more;
And mys - tic sweet com - mun - ion With those whose rest is won.

From heaven He came and sought her To be His ho - ly bride;
One ho - ly name she bless - es, Par - takes one ho - ly food,
Yet saints their watch are keep - ing; Their cry goes up - "How long?"
Till with the vi - sion glo - rious Her long - ing eyes are blest,
Oh, hap - py ones and ho - ly! Lord, give us grace that we,

With His own blood He bought her, And for her life He died.
And to one hope she press - es, With ev - ery grace en - dued.
But soon the night of weep - ing Shall be the morn of song.
And the great Church vic - to - rious Shall be the Church at rest.
Like them, the meek and low - ly, On high may dwell with Thee. A-MEN.

92 When the Roll Is Called Up Yonder

. . . so shall we ever be with the Lord. 1 Thess. 4:17

James M. Black, 1856-1938

THE ROLL 15.11.15.11. with Refrain
James M. Black, 1856-1938

1. When the trum-pet of the Lord shall sound and time shall be no more, And the
2. On that bright and cloud-less morn-ing when the dead in Christ shall rise, And the
3. Let us la - bor for the Mas-ter from the dawn to set -ting sun, Let us
morn-ing breaks e - ter - nal, bright and fair; When the saved of earth shall gath-er
glo - ry of His res - ur - rec-tion share; When His cho-sen ones shall gath-er
talk of all His won-drous love and care; Then when all of life is o - ver,
o - ver on the oth - er shore, And the roll is called up yon-der, I'll be there.
to their home be-yond the skies, And the roll is called up yon-der, I'll be there.
and our work on earth is done, And the roll is called up yon-der, We'll be there.
REFRAIN
When the roll is called up yon - der, When the
When the roll is called up yon - der, I'll be there,
roll is called up yon - der, When the roll is
When the roll is called up yon-der, I'll be there, When the roll is

When the Roll Is Called Up Yonder

called up yon - der, When the roll is called up yon- der, I'll be there.

Breathe on Me, Breath of God   93

. . . he breathed on them, and saith . . . Receive ye the Holy Ghost. John 20:22

Edwin Hatch, 1835-1889

BOYLSTON S.M.
Lowell Mason, 1792-1872

1. Breathe on me, Breath of God, Fill me with life a - new,
2. Breathe on me, Breath of God, Un - til my heart is pure,
3. Breathe on me, Breath of God, Till I am whol - ly Thine,
4. Breathe on me, Breath of God, So shall I nev - er die,

That I may love what Thou dost love, And do what Thou wouldst do.
Un - til with Thee I will one will To do or to en - dure.
Till all this earth - ly part of me Glows with Thy fire di - vine.
But live with Thee the per- fect life Of Thine e - ter - ni - ty.

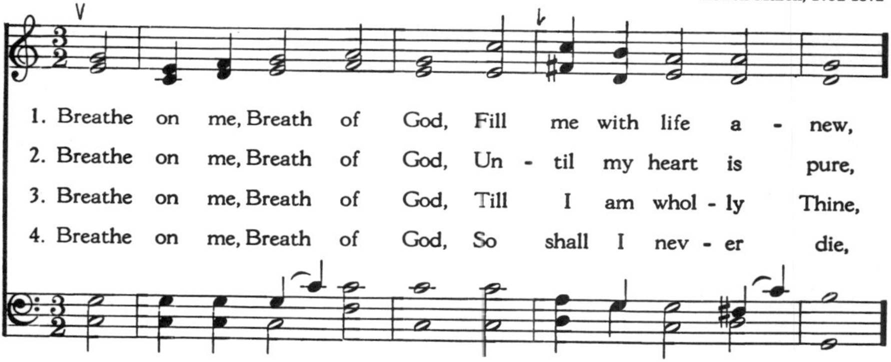

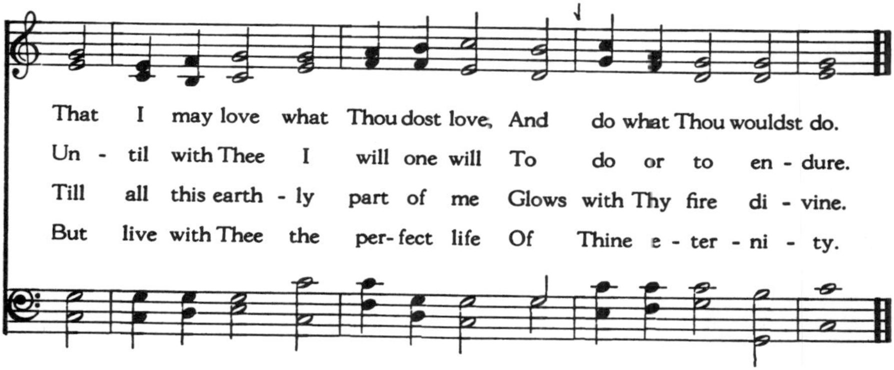

Glorious Things of Thee Are Spoken

Glorious things are spoken of thee, O city of God. . . . Psa. 87:3

AUSTRIA 8.7.8.7.D.

John Newton, 1725-1807

Franz Joseph Haydn, 1732-1809

1. Glo - rious things of thee are spo-ken, Zi - on, cit - y of our God;
2. See, the streams of liv - ing wa - ters, Spring-ing from e - ter - nal love,
3. Round each hab - i - ta - tion hov-ering, See the cloud and fire ap-pear
4. Blest in-hab - i - tants of Zi - on, Washed in the Re - deem - er's blood;
5. Sav - iour, if of Zi - on's cit - y I, through grace, a mem - ber am,

He whose word can - not be bro - ken Formed thee for His own a - bode:
Well sup - ply thy sons and daugh-ters, And all fear of want re - move:
For a glo - ry and a cov-ering, Show - ing that the Lord is near;
Je - sus, whom their souls re - ly on, Makes them kings and priests to God.
Let the world de - ride or pi - ty—I will glo - ry in Thy name.

On the Rock of A - ges found-ed, What can shake thy sure re-pose?
Who can faint, when such a riv - er Ev - er flows their thirst t' as-suage;
Thus de - riv - ing from their ban - ner Light by night, and shade by day,
'Tis His love His peo-ple rais - es O - ver self to reign as kings;
Fad - ing is the world-ling's pleas-ure, All his boast - ed pomp and show;

With sal - va - tion's walls sur - round-ed, Thou may'st smile at all thy foes.
Grace, which like the Lord, the giv - er, Nev - er fails from age to age.
Safe they feed up - on the man - na Which He gives them when they pray.
And as priests, His sol - emn prais - es, Each for a thank-of-fering brings.
Sol - id joys and last - ing treas-ure None but Zi - on's chil - dren know.

Jesus Only

... they saw no man, save Jesus only. Matt. 17:8

95

Albert B. Simpson, 1843-1919

J.H. Burke, 19th century

1. Je - sus on - ly is our mes - sage, Je - sus all our theme shall be;
2. Je - sus on - ly is our Sav - iour, All our guilt He bore a - way,
3. Je - sus is our Sanc - ti - fi - er, Cleans-ing us from self and sin,
4. Je - sus on - ly is our Heal - er, All our sick-ness - es He bear,
5. Je - sus on - ly is our pow - er, He the gift of Pen - te - cost;
6. And for Je - sus we are wait - ing, Lis-tening for the ad - vent call;

We will lift up Je - sus ev - er, Je - sus on - ly will we see.
All our right-eous - ness He gives us, All our strength from day to day.
And with all His Spir-it's full-ness, Fill-ing all our hearts with-in.
And His ris - en life and full-ness All His mem - bers still may share.
Je - sus, breathe Thy power up-on us, Fill us with the Ho - ly Ghost.
But 'twill still be Je - sus on - ly, Je - sus ev - er, all in all.

REFRAIN

Je - sus on - ly, Je - sus ev - er, Je - sus all in all we sing,

Sav-iour, Sanc - ti - fi - er, and Heal - er, Glo-rious Lord and com-ing King.

How Firm a Foundation

(FIRST TUNE)

. . . the word of the Lord endureth for ever. . . . 1 Pet. 1:25

ADESTE FIDELES 11.11.11.11. with repeat
Attributed to John F. Wade, circa 1711-1786

From John Rippon's *Selection of Hymns*, "K", 1787

As in *Cantus Diversi*, 1751

1. How firm a foun - da - tion, ye saints of the Lord, Is
2. "Fear not, I am with thee, Oh, be not dis - mayed, For
3. "When through the deep wa - ters I call thee to go, The
4. "When through fi - ery tri - als thy path - way shall lie, My
5. "The soul that on Je - sus hath leaned for re - pose, I

laid for your faith in His ex - cel - lent Word! What more can He
I am thy God, I will still give thee aid; I'll strength-en thee,
riv - ers of sor - row shall not o - ver - flow, For I will be
grace all - suf - fi - cient shall be thy sup - ply; The flame shall not
will not, I will not de - sert to his foes; That soul, though all

say than to you He hath said, To you who for ref - uge to
help thee, and cause thee to stand, Up - held by My gra - cious, om -
with thee, thy tri - als to bless, And sanc - ti - fy to thee thy
hurt thee; I on - ly de - sign Thy dross to con - sume and thy
hell should en - deav - or to shake, I'll nev - er, no nev - er, no

Je - sus have fled, To you who for ref - uge to Je - sus have fled?
nip - o - tent hand, Up - held by My gra - cious, om-nip - o - tent hand.
deep - est dis - tress, And sanc - ti - fy to thee thy deep - est dis-tress.
gold to re - fine, Thy dross to con-sume and thy gold to re - fine.
nev - er for - sake! I'll nev - er, no nev - er, no nev - er for-sake!"

Break Thou the Bread of Life

Then opened he their understanding . . . Luke 24:45

Stanzas 1-2 by Mary A. Lathbury, 1841-1913
Stanzas 3-4 by Alexander Groves, 1843-1909

LATHBURY 6.4.6.4.D
William F. Sherwin, 1826-1888

1. Break Thou the bread of life, Dear Lord, to me,
2. Bless Thou the truth, dear Lord, To me, to me,
3. Thou art the bread of life, O Lord, to me,
4. Oh, send Thy Spir - it, Lord, Now un - to me,

As Thou didst break the loaves Be - side the sea;
As Thou didst bless the bread By Gal - i - lee;
Thy ho - ly Word, the truth That sav - eth me;
That He may touch my eyes And make me see;

Be - yond the sa - cred page I seek Thee, Lord;
Then shall all bond - age cease, All fet - ters fall,
Give me to eat and live With Thee a - bove,
Show me the truth con - cealed With - in Thy Word,

My spir - it pants for Thee, O liv - ing Word.
And I shall find my peace, My all in all.
Teach me to love Thy truth For Thou art love.
And in Thy Book re - vealed, I see Thee, Lord.

Jesus Shall Reign

. . . and he shall reign forever and ever. Rev. 11:15

Isaac Watts, 1674-1748

DUKE STREET L.M.
John Hatton, circa 1710-1793

1. Je - sus shall reign wher - e'er the sun Doth his suc-
2. Be - hold, the is - lands with their kings And Eur - ope
3. To Him shall end - less prayer be made, And prais - es
4. Peo - ples and realms of ev - ery tongue Dwell on His
5. Bless - ings a - bound wher - e'er He reigns; The pris - oner
6. Let ev - ery crea - ture rise and bring Pe - cu - liar

ces - sive jour - neys run; His king - dom stretch from
her best trib - ute brings; From north to south the
throng to crown His head. His name like sweet per -
love with sweet - est song, And in - fant voic - es
leaps to loose his chains; The wea - ry find e -
hon - ors to our King. An - gels de - scend with

shore to shore, Till moons shall wax and wane no more.
princ - es meet To pay their hom - age at His feet.
fume shall rise With ev - ery morn - ing sac - ri - fice.
shall pro - claim Their ear - ly bless - ings on His name.
ter - nal rest And all the sons of want are blest.
songs a - gain And earth re - peat the long A - men.

The Call for Reapers

99

Pray . . . that he will send forth labourers into his harvest. Matt. 9:38

HARVESTTIME 8.7.8.7. with Refrain
J.B.O. Clemm, 19th century

John O. Thompson, 1782-1818

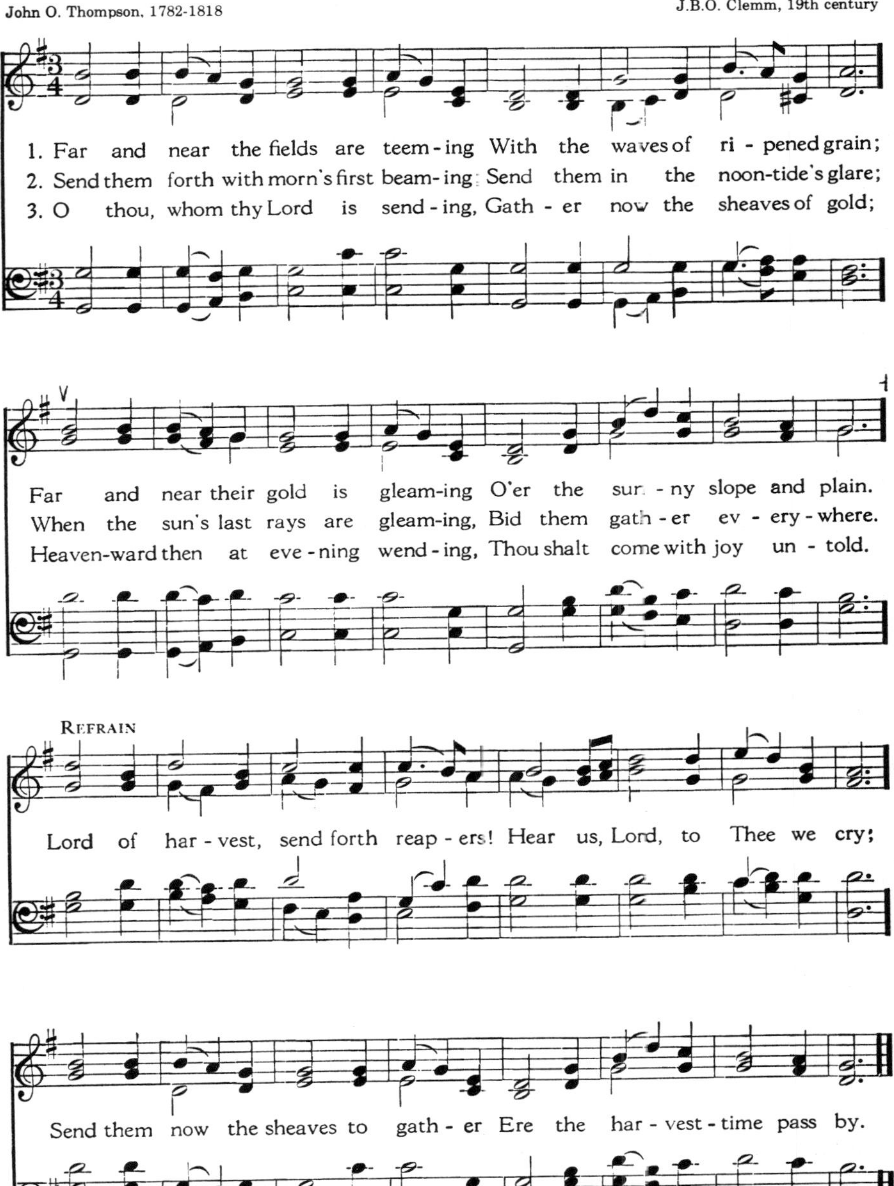

1. Far and near the fields are teem-ing With the waves of ri - pened grain;
2. Send them forth with morn's first beam-ing; Send them in the noon-tide's glare;
3. O thou, whom thy Lord is send-ing, Gath - er now the sheaves of gold;
Far and near their gold is gleam-ing O'er the sun - ny slope and plain.
When the sun's last rays are gleam-ing, Bid them gath - er ev - ery - where.
Heaven-ward then at eve - ning wend-ing, Thou shalt come with joy un - told.
REFRAIN
Lord of har - vest, send forth reap - ers! Hear us, Lord, to Thee we cry;
Send them now the sheaves to gath - er Ere the har - vest - time pass by.

Soldiers of Christ, Arise

Put on the whole armour of God . . . Eph. 6:11

Charles Wesley, 1707-1788

DIADEMATA S.M.D.
George J. Elvey, 1816-1893

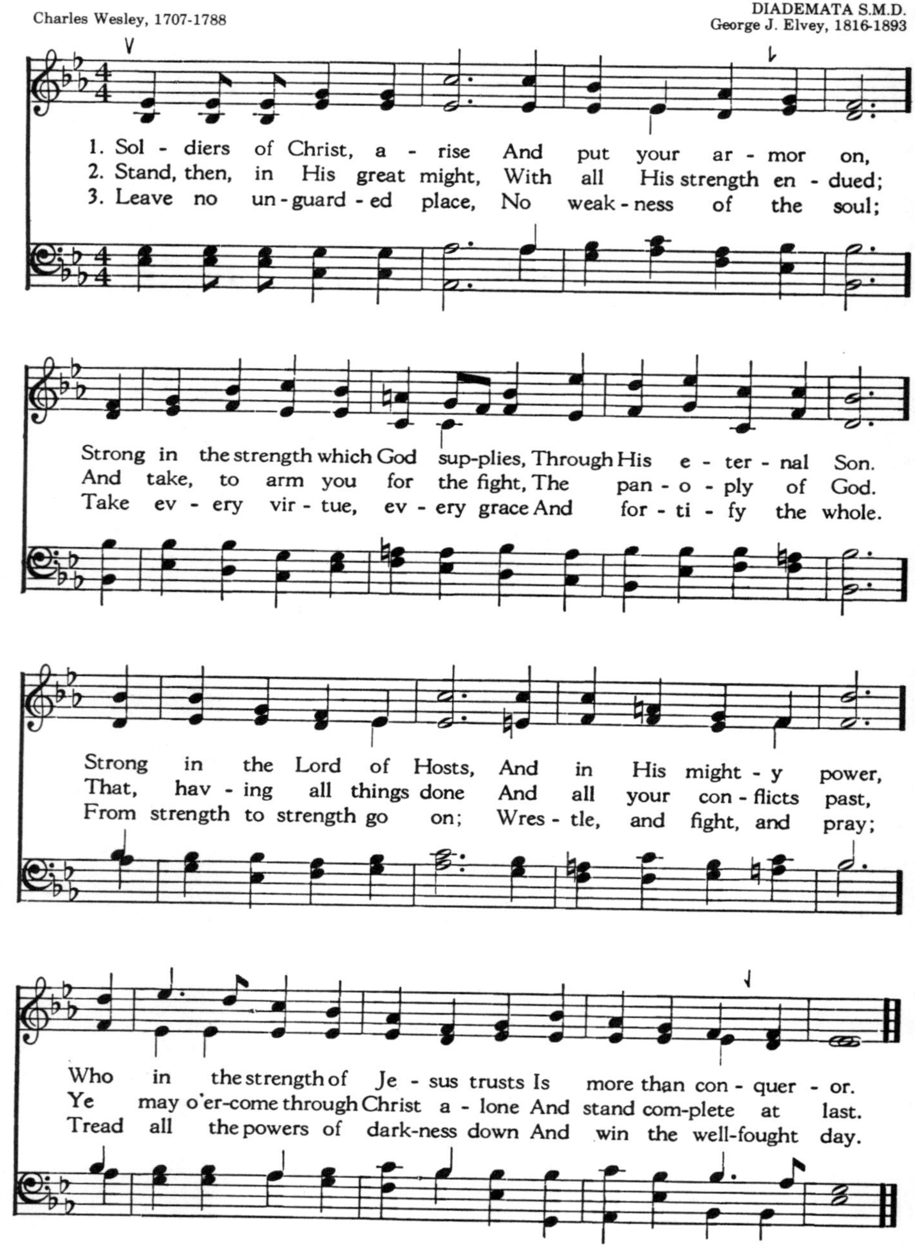

1. Sol - diers of Christ, a - rise And put your ar - mor on,
2. Stand, then, in His great might, With all His strength en - dued;
3. Leave no un - guard - ed place, No weak - ness of the soul;

Strong in the strength which God sup-plies, Through His e - ter - nal Son.
And take, to arm you for the fight, The pan - o - ply of God.
Take ev - ery vir - tue, ev - ery grace And for - ti - fy the whole.

Strong in the Lord of Hosts, And in His might - y power,
That, hav - ing all things done And all your con - flicts past,
From strength to strength go on; Wres - tle, and fight, and pray;

Who in the strength of Je - sus trusts Is more than con - quer - or.
Ye may o'er-come through Christ a - lone And stand com-plete at last.
Tread all the powers of dark-ness down And win the well-fought day.

Lead On, O King Eternal

Lead On, O King Eternal
. . . I am the Lord thy God which . . . leadeth thee . . . Isa. 48:17
Ernest W. Shurtleff, 1862-1917
LANCASHIRE 7.6.7.6.D.
Henry T. Smart, 1813-1879
1. Lead on, O King e - ter - nal, The day of march has come;
2. Lead on, O King e - ter - nal, To lands of deep - est night;
3. Lead on, O King e - ter - nal; We fol - low not with fears,
Hence-forth in fields of con - quest Thy tents shall be our home.
We fol - low where Thou lead - est As her - alds of the light.
For glad - ness breaks like morn - ing Wher - e'er Thy face ap - pears.
Through days of prep - a - ra - tion Thy grace has made us strong,
May we to souls im - mor - tal Thy Word of life con - vey
Thy cross is lift - ed o'er us; We jour - ney in its light;
And now, O King e - ter - nal, We lift our bat - tle song.
And o - pen heav - en's por - tal Through Christ the truth, the way.
The crown a - waits the con - quest; Lead on, O God of might.

O Zion, Haste

And we declare unto you glad tidings ... Acts 13:32

TIDINGS 11.10.11.10. with Refrain

Mary A. Thomson, 1834-1923

James Walch, 1837-1901

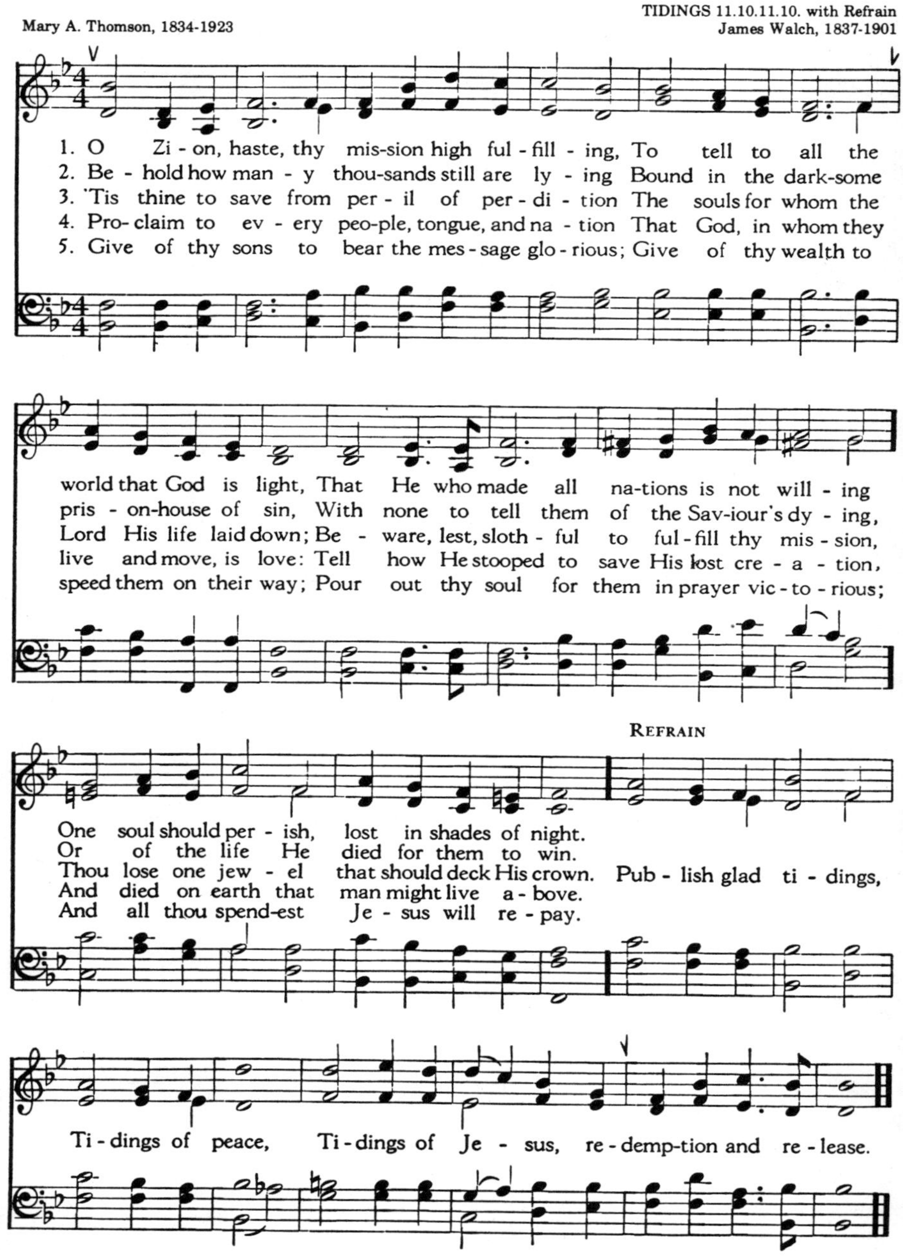

1. O Zi-on, haste, thy mis-sion high ful-fill-ing, To tell to all the
2. Be-hold how man-y thou-sands still are ly-ing Bound in the dark-some
3. 'Tis thine to save from per-il of per-di-tion The souls for whom the
4. Pro-claim to ev-ery peo-ple, tongue, and na-tion That God, in whom they
5. Give of thy sons to bear the mes-sage glo-rious; Give of thy wealth to

world that God is light, That He who made all na-tions is not will-ing
pris-on-house of sin, With none to tell them of the Sav-iour's dy-ing,
Lord His life laid down; Be-ware, lest, sloth-ful to ful-fill thy mis-sion,
live and move, is love: Tell how He stooped to save His lost cre-a-tion,
speed them on their way; Pour out thy soul for them in prayer vic-to-rious;

REFRAIN

One soul should per-ish, lost in shades of night.
Or of the life He died for them to win.
Thou lose one jew-el that should deck His crown. Pub-lish glad ti-dings,
And died on earth that man might live a-bove.
And all thou spend-est Je-sus will re-pay.

Ti-dings of peace, Ti-dings of Je-sus, re-demp-tion and re-lease.

Send the Light

O send out thy light and the truth ... Psa. 43:3

Charles H. Gabriel, 1856-1932

MCCABE 11.6.11.6. with Refrain
Charles H. Gabriel, 1856-1932

1. There's a call comes ring-ing o'er the rest-less wave, "Send the light!
2. We have heard the Mac - e - do - nian call to-day, "Send the light!
3. Let us not grow wea - ry in the work of love, Send the light!
, Send the light!

Send the light!" There are souls to res - cue, there are souls to save;
Send the light!" And a gold - en of - fer-ing at the cross we lay;
Send the light! Let us gath - er jew - els for a crown a - bove,

REFRAIN

Send the light! Send the light! Send the light, the bless-ed
Send the light!

gos - pel light; Let it shine from shore to shore; Send the light,

the bless - ed gos - pel light; Let it shine for - ev - er - more.

The Regions Beyond

Go ye therefore, and teach all nations . . . Matt. 28:19

Albert B. Simpson, 1843-1919

Margaret M. Simpson, 1876-1958

1. To the re-gions be-yond I must go, I must go, Where the sto-ry has
2. To the hard-est of plac-es He calls me to go, Not think-ing of
3. O ye that are spend-ing your lei-sure and powers In pleas-ures so
4. There are oth-er lost sheep that the Mas-ter must bring, And to them must the

nev-er been told; To the mil-lions that nev-er have heard of His love,
com-fort or ease; The world may pro-nounce me a dream-er, a fool—
fool-ish and fond, A-wake from your self-ish-ness, fol-ly, and sin
mes-sage be told. He sends me to gath-er them out of all lands

I must tell the sweet sto-ry of old.
E-nough if the Mas-ter I please. To the re - gions be-
And go to the re-gions be-yond.
And wel-come them back to His fold. I must go,

yond, I must go, I must go, Till the
I must go, To the re-gions be-yond I must go,

world, all the world, His sal-va - tion shall know.
Till the world, all the world, His sal-va-tion shall know.

Jesus Saves

. . . all the ends of the earth shall see the salvation of our God. Isa. 52:10

JESUS SAVES 7.6.7.6.7.7.7.6.
Priscilla J. Owens, 1829-1907
William J. Kirkpatrick, 1838-1921

1. We have heard the joy - ful sound: Je - sus saves! Je - sus saves!
2. Waft it on the roll - ing tide; Je - sus saves! Je - sus saves!
3. Sing a - bove the bat - tle's strife, Je - sus saves! Je - sus saves!
4. Give the winds a might - y voice, Je - sus saves! Je - sus saves!

Spread the ti - dings all a - round: Je - sus saves! Je - sus saves!
Tell to sin - ners far and wide: Je - sus saves! Je - sus saves!
By His death and end - less life, Je - sus saves! Je - sus saves!
Let the na - tions now re - joice, Je - sus saves! Je - sus saves!

Bear the news to ev - ery land, Climb the steeps and cross the waves;
Sing, ye is - lands of the sea; Ech - o back, ye o - cean caves;
Sing it soft - ly through the gloom, When the heart for mer - cy craves;
Shout sal - va - tion full and free, To each shore that o - cean laves—

On - ward—'tis our Lord's com - mand. Je - sus saves! Je - sus saves!
Earth shall keep her ju - bi - lee— Je - sus saves! Je - sus saves!
Sing in tri - umph o'er the tomb, Je - sus saves! Je - sus saves!
This our song of vic - to - ry: Je - sus saves! Je - sus saves!

A Missionary Cry

Multitudes, multitudes in the valley of decision ... Joel 3:14

Albert B. Simpson, 1843-1919

Melody by J.H. Burke, 19th century

1. A hun-dred thou-sand souls a day Are pass-ing one by one a-way In Christ-less guilt and gloom; With-out one ray of hope or light, With fu-ture dark as end-less night, They're pass-ing to their doom, They're pass-ing to their doom.
2. O Ho-ly Ghost, Thy peo-ple move, Bap-tize their hearts with faith and love And con-se-crate their gold. At Je-sus' feet their mil-lions pour, And all their ranks u-nite once more, As in the days of old, As in the days of old.
3. The Mas-ter's com-ing draw-eth near; The Son of Man will soon ap-pear; His king-dom is at hand. But ere that glo-rious day can be, This gos-pel of the king-dom we Must preach in ev-ery land, Must preach in ev-ery land.
4. Oh, let us then His com-ing haste, Oh, let us end this aw-ful waste Of souls that nev-er die. A thou-sand mil-lions still are lost; A Sav-iour's blood has paid the cost, Oh, hear their dy-ing cry, Oh, hear their dy-ing cry.
5. They're pass-ing, pass-ing fast a-way, A hun-dred thou-sand souls a day In Christ-less guilt and gloom. O Church of Christ, what wilt thou say When, in the aw-ful judg-ment day, They charge thee with their doom, They charge thee with their doom?

A Missionary Cry

REFRAIN
They're pass - ing, pass - ing fast a - way In thou - sands day by day; They're pass - ing to their doom, They're pass - ing to their doom.

Use Me Today
107
. . . serve him with a perfect heart . . . 1 Chron. 28:9
Gertrude R. Dugan, 1873-1948
George C. Stebbins, 1846-1945
1. Use me to - day, O Sav - iour di - vine! Cleanse and re -
2. Use me to - day, Lord, use e - ven me— Use me to
3. Use me to - day to scat - ter the seed, Bring - ing the
new this ser - vant of Thine. Lord, with Thy Spir - it fill me, I
lead some lost one to Thee. Lead where Thou wilt, Lord; o - pen the
bless - ing some - one may need. Wheth - er I toil or qui - et - ly
pray; Then, in Thy serv - ice, use me to - day.
way, And to Thy glo - ry, use me to - day.
pray, Bless - ed Lord Je - sus, use me to - day.

108
The Cleansing Wave
. . . there shall be a fountain opened . . . for sin and for uncleanness. Zech. 13:1
Phoebe P. Knapp, 1839-1908
Phoebe P. Knapp, 1839-1908

1. Oh, now I see the cleans-ing wave! The foun-tain deep and wide;
2. I rise to walk in heaven's own light A - bove the world of sin,
3. A - maz-ing grace! 'Tis heaven be - low To feel the blood ap -plied,

Je - sus, my Lord, might - y to save, Points to His wound-ed side.
With heart made pure and gar-ments white, With Christ en-throned with - in.
And Je - sus, on - ly Je - sus know—My Je - sus cru - ci - fied.

REFRAIN
The cleans-ing stream I see, I see; I plunge, and, oh, it cleans-eth me!

Oh, praise the Lord, it cleans-eth me! It cleans-eth me— yes, cleans-eth me.

At Calvary

... Calvary, there they crucified him ... Luke 23:33

CALVARY 9.9.9.4. with Refrain

William R. Newell, 1868-1956

Daniel B. Towner, 1850-1919

1. Years I spent in van-i-ty and pride, Car-ing
2. By God's Word at last my sin I learned; Then I
3. Now I've given to Je-sus ev-ery-thing; Now I
4. Oh, the love that drew sal-va-tion's plan! Oh, the

not my Lord was cru-ci-fied, Know-ing not it was for
trem-bled at the law I'd spurned Till my guilt-y soul im-
glad-ly own Him as my King; Now my rap-tured soul can
grace that brought it down to man! Oh, the might-y gulf that

REFRAIN

me He died On Cal-va-ry.
plor-ing turned To Cal-va-ry.
on-ly sing Of Cal-va-ry.
God did span At Cal-va-ry!

Mer-cy there was great, and

grace was free; Par-don there was mul-ti-plied to me;

There my bur-dened soul found lib-er-ty— At Cal-va-ry.

110 Saved by the Blood

. . . by his own blood he . . . obtained eternal redemption for us. Heb. 9:12

GLORY I'M SAVED 10.11.11.10. with Refrain

S.J. Henderson, 19th century

Melody by Daniel B. Towner, 1850-1919

1. Saved by the blood of the cru - ci - fied One! Now ran - somed from
2. Saved by the blood of the cru - ci - fied One! The an - gels re -
3. Saved by the blood of the cru - ci - fied One! The Fa - ther He
4. Saved by the blood of the cru - ci - fied One! All hail to the

sin and a new work be - gun, Sing praise to the Fa - ther and
joic - ing be - cause it is done; A child of the Fa - ther, joint
spake, and His will it was done; Great price of my par - don, His
Fa - ther, all hail to the Son, All hail to the Spir - it—the

praise to the Son, Saved by the blood of the cru - ci - fied One!
heir with the Son, Saved by the blood of the cru - ci - fied One!
own pre - cious Son; Saved by the blood of the cru - ci - fied One!
great Three - in - One! Saved by the blood of the cru - ci - fied One!

REFRAIN

Saved! Saved! My sins are all par-doned, my guilt is all gone!
Glo - ry, I'm saved! Glo-ry I'm saved!

Saved! Saved! I am saved by the blood of the cru - ci-fied One!
Glo-ry, I'm saved! Glo-ry, I'm saved!

Since I Have Been Redeemed

. . . I will exalt thee, I will praise thy name . . . Isa. 25:1

111

Edwin O. Excell, 1851-1921

OTHELLO C.M. with Refrain
Melody by Edwin O. Excell, 1851-1921

1. I have a song I love to sing, Since I have been re - deemed,
2. I have a Christ that sat - is - fies, Since I have been re - deemed,
3. I have a wit - ness bright and clear, Since I have been re - deemed,
4. I have a joy I can't ex - press, Since I have been re - deemed,
5. I have a home pre - pared for me, Since I have been re - deemed,

Of my Re - deem - er, Sav - iour, King— Since I have been re - deemed.
To do His will my high - est prize— Since I have been re - deemed.
Dis - pell - ing ev - ery doubt and fear— Since I have been re - deemed.
All through His blood and right - eous - ness— Since I have been re - deemed.
Where I shall dwell e - ter - nal - ly— Since I have been re - deemed.

REFRAIN

Since I have been re - deemed, Since I have been re-deemed,
Since I have been re-deemed, since I have been re-deemed,

I will glo - ry in His name; Since I have been re -
Since I have been re-deemed, since

deemed, I will glo - ry in the Sav - iour's name.
I have been re-deemed,

My Redeemer

Who gave himself for us, that he might redeem us . . . Titus 2:14

Philip P. Bliss, 1838-1876

MY REDEEMER 8.7.8.7. with Refrain
James McGranahan, 1840-1907

1. I will sing of my Re-deem-er And His won-drous love to me;
2. I will tell the won-drous sto-ry, How my lost es-tate to save,
3. I will sing of my Re-deem-er, And His heaven-ly love for me;

On the cru-el cross He suf-fered, From the curse to set me free.
In His bound-less love and mer-cy, He the ran-som free-ly gave.
He from death to life hath brought me, Son of God with Him to be.

REFRAIN

Sing, oh, sing of my Re-deem-er,
of my Re-deem-er, Sing, oh, sing of my Re-deem-er,

With His blood He pur-chased me,
He pur-chased me, With His blood He pur-chased me,

On the cross He sealed my par-don,
He sealed my par-don, On the cross He sealed my par-don,

My Redeemer

Paid the debt, and made me free.
and made me free, and made me free.

Glory to His Name

113

... unto thy name give glory ... Psa. 115:1

Elisha A. Hoffman, 1839-1929

GLORY TO HIS NAME 9.9.9.5. with Refrain
John H. Stockton, 1813-1877

1. Down at the cross where my Sav-iour died, Down where for cleans-ing from
2. I am so won-drous-ly saved from sin; Je - sus so sweet-ly a-
3. Oh, pre-cious foun-tain that saves from sin! I am so glad I have
4. Come to this foun-tain so rich and sweet; Cast thy poor soul at the

sin I cried—There to my heart was the blood ap-plied; Glo-ry to His name!
bides with-in, There at the cross where He took me in; Glo-ry to His name!
en-tered in; There Je-sus saves me and keeps me clean; Glo-ry to His name!
Sav-iour's feet; Plunge in to-day and be made com-plete; Glo-ry to His name!

REFRAIN
Glo - ry to His name, Glo - ry to His name;

There to my heart was the blood ap - plied; Glo - ry to His name!

Saved, Saved, Saved

. . . according to his mercy he saved us . . . Titus 3:5

Oswald J. Smith, b. 1890

HICKMAN 9.9.9.9. with Refrain
Roger M. Hickman, 1888-1968

1. Saved! saved! saved! my sins are all for - given; Christ is
2. Saved! saved! saved! by grace and grace a - lone; Oh, what
3. Saved! saved! saved! O joy be - yond com - pare! Christ my

mine! I'm on my way to heaven; Once a guilt - y
won - drous love to me was shown, In my stead Christ
life and I His con - stant care; Yield - ing all and

sin - ner, lost, un - done, Now a child of God, saved through His Son.
Je - sus bled and died, Bore my sins, for me was cru - ci - fied.
trust - ing Him a - lone, Liv - ing now each mo - ment as His own.

REFRAIN

Saved! I'm saved through Christ, my all in all; Saved! I'm saved, what-
my all in all;

ev - er may be - fall; He died up - on the cross for me, He bore the aw - ful

Saved, Saved, Saved
pen - al - ty; And now I'm saved e - ter - nal - ly, I'm saved! saved! saved!

Satisfied
115
For he satisfieth the longing soul . . . Psa. 107:9
SATISFIED 8.7.8.7. with Refrain
Ralph E. Hudson, 1843-1901
Clara T. Williams, 1858-1937

1. All my life long I had pant - ed For a drink from some cool spring
2. Feed - ing on the husks a - round me Till my strength was al - most gone,
3. Poor I was, and sought for rich - es, Some-thing that would sat - is - fy;
4. Well of wa - ter, ev - er spring-ing, Bread of life, so rich and free.

That I hoped would quench the burn-ing Of the thirst I felt with - in.
Longed my soul for some-thing bet - ter, On - ly still to hun - ger on.
But the dust I gath-ered round me On - ly mocked my soul's sad cry.
Un - told wealth that nev - er fail - eth, My Re - deem - er is to me.

REFRAIN
Hal - le - lu - jah! I have found Him Whom my soul so long has craved!

Je - sus sat - is - fies my long-ings; Through His blood I now am saved.

He Lives

. . . he is risen; he is not here . . . Mark 16:6

ACKLEY Irregular with Refrain
Alfred H. Ackley, 1887-1960

Alfred H. Ackley, 1887-1960

1. I serve a ris - en Sav - iour, He's in the world to - day;
2. In all the world a - round me I see His lov - ing care,
3. Re - joice, re - joice, O Chris - tian, lift up your voice and sing

I know that He is liv - ing, what - ev - er men may say;
And though my heart grows wea - ry, I nev - er will de - spair;
E - ter - nal hal - le - lu - jahs to Je - sus Christ the King!

I see His hand of mer - cy, I hear His voice of cheer;
I know that He is lead - ing through all the storm - y blast;
The hope of all who seek Him, the help of all who find,

And just the time I need Him He's al - ways near.
The day of His ap - pear - ing will come at last.
None oth - er is so lov - ing, so good and kind.

He Lives

REFRAIN
He lives, He lives, Christ Je - sus lives to - day!
He lives, He lives,
He walks with me and talks with me a - long life's nar - row way.
He lives, He lives, sal - va - tion to im - part!
He lives, He lives,
You ask me how I know He lives? He lives with - in my heart.

My Faith Has Found a Resting Place

. . . in that, while we were yet sinners, Christ died for us. Rom. 5:8

LANDAS C.M. with Refrain
Norse Air
Lidie H. Edmunds, 19th century
Arranged by William J. Kirkpatrick, 1838-1921

1. My faith has found a rest - ing place, Not in de - vice nor creed;
2. E - nough for me that Je - sus saves—This ends my fear and doubt;
3. My heart is lean - ing on the Word, The writ - ten Word of God,
4. My great Phy - si - cian heals the sick, The lost He came to save;
I trust the ev - er - liv - ing One, His wounds for me shall plead.
A sin - ful soul I come to Him, He'll nev - er cast me out.
Sal - va - tion by my Sav-iour's name, Sal - va-tion through His blood.
For me His pre - cious blood He shed, For me His life He gave.
REFRAIN
I need no oth - er ar - gu - ment, I need no oth - er plea;
It is e-nough that Je - sus died, And that He died for me.

He Is Lord

118

He Is Lord
118
HE IS LORD Irregular
Anonymous
From Philippians 2:10-11
He is Lord, He is Lord! He is ris - en from the dead, and He is Lord!
Ev-ery knee shall bow, ev - ery tongue con-fess that Je - sus Christ is Lord.

I Am Not Skilled to Understand
119
. . . the Lord give thee understanding in all things. 2 Tim. 2:7
GREENWELL 8.8.8.7.
William J. Kirkpatrick, 1838-1921
Dora Greenwell, 1821-1882
1. I am not skilled to un - der - stand What
2. I take Him at His Word in - deed: "Christ
3. That He should leave His place on high And
4. And, oh, that He ful - filled may see The
5. Yes, liv - ing, dy - ing, let me bring My
God hath willed, what God hath planned; I on - ly know at
died for sin - ners"—this I read; For in my heart I
come for sin - ful man to die, You count it strange? So
trav - ail of His soul in me, And with His work con -
strength, my sol - ace from this spring— That He who lives to
His right hand Is One who is my Sav - iour!
find a need Of Him to be my Sav - iour!
once did I Be - fore I knew my Sav - iour!
tent - ed be, As I with my dear Sav - iour!
be my King Once died to be my Sav - iour!

I Am Not Skilled to Understand

119

120   Nothing But the Blood

. . . being now justified by his blood, we shall be saved . . . Rom. 5:9

Robert Lowry, 1826-1899

PLAINFIELD 7.8.7.8. with Refrain
Robert Lowry, 1826-1899

1. What can wash a-way my sin? Noth-ing but the blood of Je - sus;
2. For my par-don this I see— Noth-ing but the blood of Je - sus;
3. Noth-ing can for sin a-tone— Noth-ing but the blood of Je - sus;
4. This is all my hope and peace—Noth-ing but the blood of Je - sus;
What can make me whole a-gain? Noth-ing but the blood of Je - sus.
For my cleans-ing, this my plea— Noth-ing but the blood of Je - sus.
Naught of good that I have done— Noth-ing but the blood of Je - sus.
This is all my right-eous-ness— Noth-ing but the blood of Je - sus.
REFRAIN
Oh, pre-cious is the flow That makes me white as snow;
No oth-er fount I know, Noth-ing but the blood of Je - sus.

Hallelujah for the Cross

But God forbid that I should glory, save in the cross ... Gal 6:14

KINSMAN 6.8.6.8.6.6.6.7. with Refrain

Horatius Bonar, 1808-1889

James McGranahan, 1840-1907

1. The cross it stand-eth fast, Hal-le-lu-jah! Hal-le-lu-jah! De-fy-ing
2. It is the old cross still, Hal-le-lu-jah! Hal-le-lu-jah! Its tri-umph
3. 'Twas here the debt was paid, Hal-le-lu-jah! Hal-le-lu-jah! Our sins on

ev-ery blast, Hal-le-lu-jah! Hal-le-lu-jah! The winds of hell have blown, The
let us tell, Hal-le-lu-jah! Hal-le-lu-jah! The grace of God here shone Through
Je-sus laid, Hal-le-lu-jah! Hal-le-lu-jah! So round the cross we sing Of

world its hate hath shown, Yet it is not o-ver-thrown, Hal-le-lu-jah for the cross!
Christ the bless-ed Son, Who did for sin a-tone, Hal-le-lu-jah for the cross!
Christ, our of-fer-ing, Of Christ, our liv-ing King, Hal-le-lu-jah for the cross!

REFRAIN
Hal-le-lu-jah, hal-le-lu-jah, hal-le-lu-jah for the cross;

Hal-le-lu-jah, hal-le-lu-jah, it shall nev-er suf-fer loss!

The Great Physician

122

Who forgiveth all thine iniquities; who healeth all thy diseases. Psa. 103:3

William Hunter, 1811-1877

GREAT PHYSICIAN 8.7.8.7. with Refrain
Melody by John H. Stockton, 1813-1877

1. The great Phy-si-cian now is near, The sym-pa-thiz-ing Je-sus;
2. Your man-y sins are all for-given—Oh, hear the voice of Je-sus;
3. All glo-ry to the dy-ing Lamb, I now be-lieve in Je-sus;
4. His name dis-pels my guilt and fear, No oth-er name but Je-sus;

He speaks the droop-ing heart to cheer—Oh, hear the voice of Je-sus.
Go on your way in peace to heaven And wear a crown with Je-sus.
I love the bless-ed Sav-iour's name, I love the name of Je-sus.
Oh, how my soul de-lights to hear The charm-ing name of Je-sus.

REFRAIN

Sweet-est note in ser-aph song, Sweet-est name on mor-tal tongue,

Sweet-est car-ol ev-er sung— Je-sus, bless-ed Je-sus.

He Is Able to Deliver Thee

. . . our God . . . is able to deliver us . . . Dan. 3:17

William A. Ogden, 1841-1897

William A. Ogden, 1841-1897

1. 'Tis the grand-est theme through the a - ges rung; 'Tis the grand-est theme for a
2. 'Tis the grand-est theme in the earth or main; 'Tis the grand-est theme for a
3. 'Tis the grand-est theme, let the ti-dings roll To the guilt-y heart, to the

mor-tal tongue; 'Tis the grand-est theme that the world e'er sung—"Our God is
mor-tal strain; 'Tis the grand-est theme, tell the world a-gain—"Our God is
sin-ful soul; Look to God in faith, He will make thee whole—"Our God is

REFRAIN
a - ble to de - liv - er thee." He is a - ble to de - liv - er thee,

He is a - ble to de - liv - er thee; Though by sin op-pressed,

Go to Him for rest—"Our God is a - ble to de - liv - er thee."

A Revival Hymn

... O Lord, revive thy work ... Hab. 3:2

Oswald J. Smith, b. 1890

Bentley D. Ackley, 1872-1958

1. Re - vive Thy work, O Lord! And man - i - fest Thy power;
2. Re - vive Thy work, O Lord! And ev - ery soul in - spire;
3. Re - vive Thy work, O Lord! And give a - bound - ing joy;
4. Re - vive Thy work, O Lord! And make Thy ser - vants bold;
5. Re - vive Thy work, O Lord! Ful - fill Thy prom - ise true;
Thy work, O Lord!

Oh, come up - on Thy church and give A pen - i - ten - tial shower!
Oh, kin - dle in each heart, we pray, The Pen - te - cos - tal fire!
Oh, fill our hearts with per - fect love And burn out all al - loy!
Con - vict of sin and work once more As in the days of old.
Let Je - sus Christ be glo - ri - fied And great things for us do.

REFRAIN
Re - vive Thy work, O Lord, Come now and an - swer prayer;
an-swer prayer;

Oh, come in Ho - ly Spir - it power And save men ev - ery - where.

Grace Greater Than Our Sin

... where sin abounded, grace did much more abound. Rom. 5:20

Julia H. Johnston, 1849-1919

MOODY 9.9.9.9. with Refrain
Daniel B. Towner, 1850-1919

125

1. Mar - vel - ous grace of our lov - ing Lord, Grace that ex - ceeds our
2. Sin and de - spair, like the sea waves cold, Threat-en the soul with
3. Dark is the stain that we can - not hide, What can a - vail to
4. Mar - vel - ous, in - fi - nite, match - less grace Free - ly be-stowed on

sin and our guilt, Yon - der on Cal - va - ry's mount out - poured,
in - fi - nite loss; Grace that is great - er, yes, grace un - told,
wash it a - way? Look! There is flow - ing a crim - son tide;
all who be - lieve; You that are long - ing to see His face,

There where the blood of the Lamb was spilt.
Points to the ref - uge, the might - y cross.
Whit - er than snow you may be to - day.
Will you this mo - ment His grace re - ceive?

REFRAIN

Grace, grace, God's grace, Grace that will par - don and cleanse with - in; Grace,
Mar - vel - ous grace, in - fi - nite grace, Mar - vel - ous

grace, God's grace, Grace that is great - er than all our sin.
grace, in - fi - nite grace,

Trust and Obey

. . . if ye will obey . . . ye shall be a peculiar treasure unto me . . . Exod. 19:5

John H. Sammis, 1846-1919

TRUST AND OBEY 6.6.9.D. with Refrain
Daniel B. Towner, 1850-1919

1. When we walk with the Lord In the light of His Word, What a glo-ry He
2. Not a shad-ow can rise, Not a cloud in the skies, But His smile quick-ly
3. But we nev-er can prove The de-lights of His love Un-til all on the
4. Then in fel-low-ship sweet We will sit at His feet, Or we'll walk by His

sheds on our way! While we do His good will, He a-bides with us still
drives it a-way; Not a doubt nor a fear, Not a sigh nor a tear
al-tar we lay; For the fa-vor He shows And the joy He be-stows
side in the way; What He says we will do, Where He sends we will go—

REFRAIN

And with all who will trust and o-bey.
Can a-bide while we trust and o-bey. Trust and o-bey, for there's no oth-er
Are for them who will trust and o-bey.
Nev-er fear, on-ly trust and o-bey.

way To be hap-py in Je-sus, But to trust and o-bey.

Jesus, I Come

In the day of my trouble I sought the Lord ... Psa. 77:2

William T. Sleeper, 1819-1904

JESUS, I COME Irregular
George C. Stebbins, 1846-1945

1. Out of my bond-age, sor-row, and night, Je-sus, I come, Je-sus, I come;
2. Out of my shame-ful fail-ure and loss, Je-sus, I come, Je-sus, I come;
3. Out of un-rest and ar-ro-gant pride, Je-sus, I come, Je-sus, I come;
4. Out of the fear and dread of the tomb, Je-sus, I come, Je-sus, I come;

In - to Thy free-dom, glad-ness, and light, Je-sus, I come to Thee;
In - to the glo-rious gain of Thy cross, Je-sus, I come to Thee;
In - to Thy bless-ed will to a-bide, Je-sus, I come to Thee;
In - to the joy and light of my home, Je-sus, I come to Thee;

Out of my sick-ness in-to Thy health, Out of my want and in-to Thy wealth,
Out of earth's sor-rows in-to Thy balm, Out of life's storms and in-to Thy calm,
Out of my-self to dwell in Thy love, Out of de-spair in-to rap-tures a-bove,
Out of the depths of ru-in un-told, In-to the peace of Thy shel-ter-ing fold,

Out of my sin and in-to Thy-self, Je-sus, I come to Thee.
Out of dis-tress to ju-bi-lant psalm, Je-sus, I come to Thee.
Up-ward for aye on wings like a dove, Je-sus, I come to Thee.
Ev-er Thy glo-rious face to be-hold, Je-sus, I come to Thee.

My Trust

. . . it is required in stewards, that a man be found faithful. 1 Cor. 4:2

Albert B. Simpson, 1843-1919

Albert B. Simpson, 1843-1919

1. Lord, Thou hast given to me a trust, A high and ho-ly
2. Thou hast com-mand-ed us to go; Oh, nev-er let our
3. We all are debt-ors to our race; God holds us bound to

dis-pen-sa-tion, To tell the world, and tell I must, The
hearts be-tray Thee; And Thou hast left an aw-ful woe On
one an-oth-er; The gifts and bless-ings of His grace Were

sto-ry of Thy great sal-va-tion; Thou might'st have sent from
all who light-ly dis-o-bey Thee; Oh, let us feel and
giv-en thee to give thy broth-er; We owe to ev-ery

heaven a-bove An-gel-ic hosts to tell the sto-ry, But, in Thy
fear that woe As we would guard our own sal-va-tion, And let us
child of sin One chance, at least, for hope of heav-en; Oh, by the

My Trust

con - de - scend-ing love, On men Thou hast con-ferred the glo - ry.
an - swer to that "Go," As wit - ness - es in ev - ery na - tion.
love that brought us in, Let help and hope to them be giv - en.
REFRAIN
Let me be faith - ful to my trust, Tell - ing the world the sto - ry;
Press on my heart the woe; Put in my feet the go;
Let me be faith - ful to my trust And use me for Thy glo - ry.

Great Is Thy Faithfulness

... his compassions fail not. They are new every morning ... Lam. 3:22-23

Thomas O. Chisholm, 1866-1960

FAITHFULNESS 11.10.11.10. with Refrain
William M. Runyan, 1870-1957

1. Great is Thy faith - ful - ness, O God my Fa - ther,
2. Sum - mer and win - ter, and spring - time and har - vest,
3. Par - don for sin and a peace that en - dur - eth,

There is no shad - ow of turn - ing with Thee;
Sun, moon, and stars in their cours - es a - bove
Thy own dear pres - ence to cheer and to guide,

Thou chang - est not, Thy com - pas - sions they fail not;
Join with all na - ture in man - i - fold wit - ness
Strength for to - day and bright hope for to - mor - row—

As Thou hast been Thou for - ev - er wilt be.
To Thy great faith - ful - ness, mer - cy, and love.
Bless - ings all mine, with ten thou - sand be - side!

Great Is Thy Faithfulness

REFRAIN
Great is Thy faith - ful - ness! Great is Thy faith - ful - ness!
Morn - ing by morn - ing new mer - cies I see;
All I have need - ed Thy hand hath pro - vid - ed—
Great is Thy faith - ful - ness, Lord, un - to me!

Pass Me Not

. . . let thine ears be attentive to the voice of my supplications. Psa. 130:2

Fanny J. Crosby, 1820-1915

PASS ME NOT 8.5.8.5. with Refrain
William H. Doane, 1832-1915

1. Pass me not, O gen-tle Sav-iour, Hear my hum-ble cry;
2. Let me at the throne of mer-cy Find a sweet re-lief;
3. Trust-ing on-ly in Thy mer-it, Would I seek Thy face;
4. Thou, the Spring of all my com-fort, More than life to me,

While on oth-ers Thou art call-ing, Do not pass me by.
Kneel-ing there in deep con-tri-tion, Help my un-be-lief.
Heal my wound-ed, bro-ken spir-it, Save me by Thy grace.
Whom have I on earth be-side Thee? Whom in heaven but Thee?

REFRAIN

Sav-iour, Sav-iour, Hear my hum-ble cry; While on

oth-ers Thou art call-ing, Do not pass me by.

Lord, in This Urgent Hour

Dwight Hall

Dwight Hall

Lord, in this ur- gent hour, We long to
see thy pow'r; Send forth a migh- ty show'r
of ho- ly love. Mil-lions are lost from Thee,
Great God of ma- jes- ty, Oh, Sav- ior,
set them free, Great God of love.

Because He Lives

1 God sent His Son, they called Him Je - sus; He came to love,
2 How sweet to hold a new-born ba - by, And feel the pride,
3 And then one day I'll cross the riv - er; I'll fight life's fi -

1 heal, and for - give; He lived and died to buy my
2 and joy He gives; But great - er still the calm as -
3 nal war with pain; And then as death gives way to

1 par-don, An emp - ty grave is there to prove my Sav - ior lives.
2 sur-ance, This child can face un - cer-tain days be-cause He lives.
3 vic-tory, I'll see the lights of glo - ry and I'll know He lives.

Be-cause He lives I can face to - mor-row; Be-cause He lives

all fear is gone; Be-cause I know He holds the

fu-ture. And life is worth the liv - ing just be-cause He lives.

He Touched Me

Words & Music by
William J. Gaither

C   F   C
1. Shack - led by a heav - y bur-den,__ 'Neath a load of
2. Since I met this bless - ed Sav-iour,__ Since He cleansed and

E F   Bb   F   F#°
guilt and shame;__ Then the hand of Je - sus touched me,__ And
made me whole;__ I will nev - er cease to praise Him,__ I'll

C   F   CHORUS C
now I am no long - er the same.__ He touched me,__ Oh,__ He
shout it while e - ter - ni - ty rolls.__

F   Bb   F   D   G7   C7   F
touched me,__ and Oh, the joy that floods my soul;__ Some-thing

C7   F7   Bb   F   D   G7   C7 F
hap-pened, and now I know, He touched me and made__ me whole.__

The Star-Spangled Banner

Through God we shall do valiantly: for he it is that shall tread down our enemies. Psa. 60:12

Francis Scott Key, 1779-1843

NATIONAL ANTHEM Irregular
Attributed to John S. Smith, 1750-1836

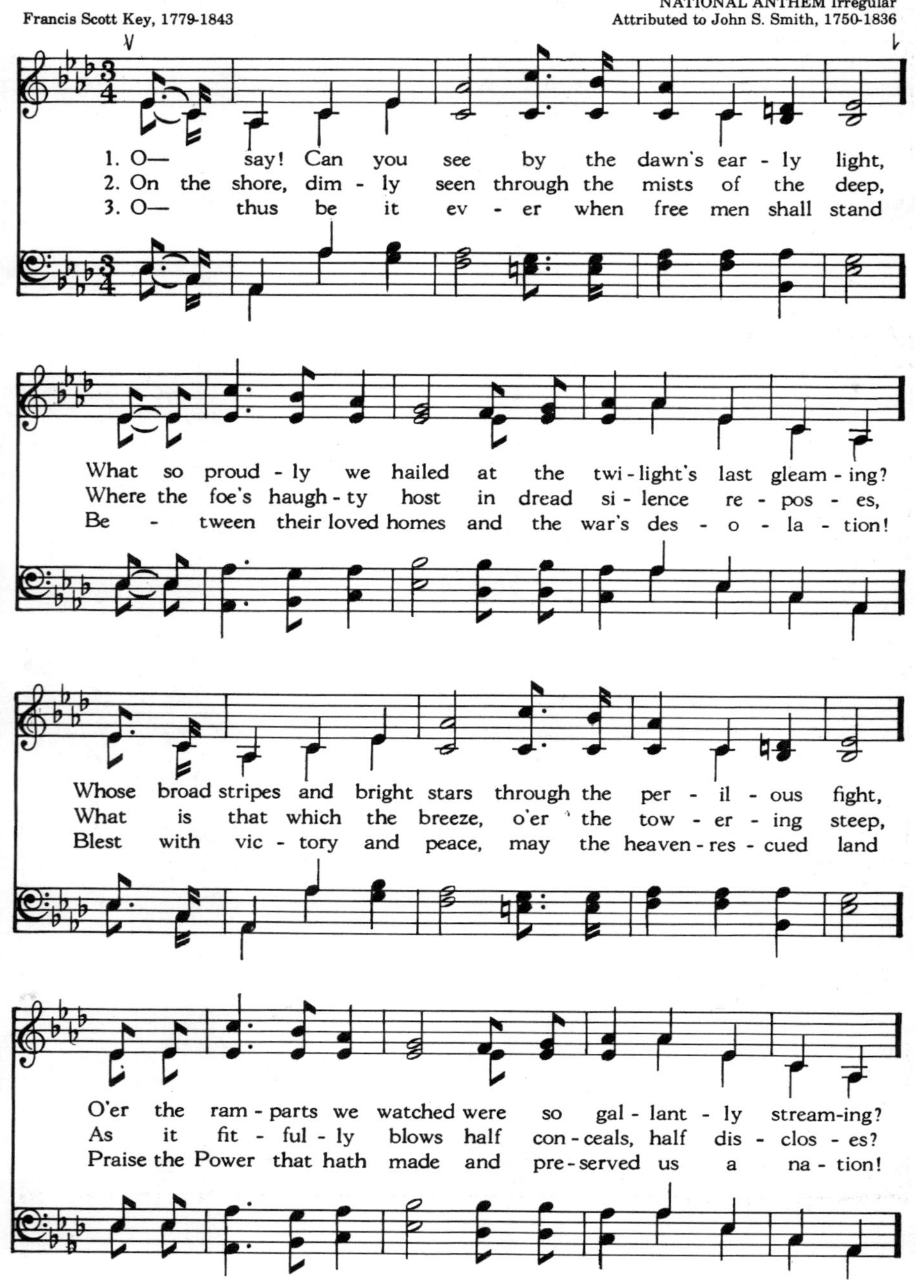

1. O— say! Can you see by the dawn's ear - ly light,
2. On the shore, dim - ly seen through the mists of the deep,
3. O— thus be it ev - er when free men shall stand
What so proud - ly we hailed at the twi - light's last gleam - ing?
Where the foe's haugh - ty host in dread si - lence re - pos - es,
Be - tween their loved homes and the war's des - o - la - tion!
Whose broad stripes and bright stars through the per - il - ous fight,
What is that which the breeze, o'er the tow - er - ing steep,
Blest with vic - tory and peace, may the heaven - res - cued land
O'er the ram - parts we watched were so gal - lant - ly stream-ing?
As it fit - ful - ly blows half con - ceals, half dis - clos - es?
Praise the Power that hath made and pre - served us a na - tion!

The Star-Spangled Banner

And the rock - et's red glare, the bomb burst - ing in air
Now it catch - es the gleam of the morn - ing's first beam,
Then con - quer we must, when our cause it is just,
Gave proof through the night that our flag was still there.
In full glo - ry re - flect - ed now shines on the stream,
And this be our mot - to: "In God is our trust!"
O— say, does that Star - Span-gled Ban - ner yet wave
'Tis the Star - Span - gled Ban - ner— O long may it wave
And the Star - Span - gled Ban - ner in tri - umph shall wave
O'er the land of the free and the home of the brave?
O'er the land of the free and the home of the brave!
O'er the land of the free and the home of the brave!

O Canada

Blessed is the nation whose God is the Lord ... Psa. 33:12

R. Stanley Weir, 1856-1926

Melody by Calixa Lavallée, 1842-1891

1. O Can - a - da! Our home and na - tive land! True pa - triot
2. O Can - a - da! Where pines and ma - ples grow, Great prair - ies
3. O Can - a - da, be-neath thy shin - ing skies May stal - wart
4. Rul - er Su - preme, who hear - est hum-ble prayer, Hold our Do -

love in all thy sons com - mand. With glow - ing hearts we
spread and lord - ly riv - ers flow, How dear to us Thy
sons and gen - tle maid - ens rise To keep thee stead - fast
min - ion in thy lov - ing care; Help us to find, O

see thee rise, The True North, strong and free, From far and
broad do - main, From East to West - ern Sea Thou land of-
through the years From East to West - ern Sea, Our own be -
God, in Thee A last - ing, rich re - ward, As, wait - ing

wide, O Can - a - da, We stand on guard for thee.
hope for all who toil! Thou True North, strong and free.
lov - ed na - tive land, Our True North, strong and free.
for the bet - ter day, We ev - er stand on guard.

O Canada

REFRAIN
God keep our land, glo - rious and free ! O Can - a - da, we
stand on guard for thee. O Can - a - da, we stand on guard for thee.

God Save the Queen 136

Remember them which have the rule over you . . . Heb. 13:7

NATIONAL ANTHEM 6.6.4.6.6.6.4.
From *Thesaurus Musicus*, circa 1740

Anonymous, 18th century

1. God save our gra - cious Queen! Long live our no - ble Queen!
2. Thy choic - est gifts in store, On her be pleased to pour,
God save the Queen! Send her vic - to - ri - ous, Hap - py and
Long may she reign. May she de - fend our laws, And ev - er
glo - ri - ous, Long to reign o - ver us, God save the Queen!
give us cause To sing with heart and voice, God save the Queen!

137
America, the Beautiful
Blessed is the nation whose God is the Lord . . . Psa. 33:12
Katherine L. Bates, 1859-1929
MATERNA C.M.D.
Samuel A. Ward, 1847-1903

1. O beau - ti - ful for spa - cious skies, For am - ber waves of grain,
2. O beau - ti - ful for pil - grim feet, Whose stern, im - pas-sioned stress
3. O beau - ti - ful for he - roes proved In lib - er - at - ing strife,
4. O beau - ti - ful for pa - triot dream That sees be - yond the years

For pur - ple moun-tain maj - es - ties A - bove the fruit - ed plain!
A thor - ough-fare for free - dom beat A - cross the wil - der - ness!
Who more than self their coun - try loved, And mer - cy more than life!
Thine al - a - bas - ter cit - ies gleam, Un-dimmed by hu - man tears!

A - mer - i - ca! A - mer - i - ca! God shed His grace on thee,
A - mer - i - ca! A - mer - i - ca! God mend thine ev - ery flaw,
A - mer - i - ca! A - mer - i - ca! May God thy gold re - fine
A - mer - i - ca! A - mer - i - ca! God shed His grace on thee

And crown thy good with broth - er - hood From sea to shin - ing sea!
Con - firm thy soul in self - con-trol, Thy lib - er - ty in law!
Till all suc - cess be no - ble-ness And ev - ery gain di - vine!
And crown thy good with broth - er - hood From sea to shin - ing sea! A-MEN.

INDEX OF TITLES